Myth of the Nativity
The Virgin Birth Re-examined

Andrew Welburn

Myth of the Nativity
The Virgin Birth Re-examined

Floris Books

First published in 2006 by Floris Books
© 2006 Andrew Welburn

British Library CIP Data available

ISBN-10 0-86315-543-X
ISBN-13 978-086315-543-7

Printed in Great Britain
By Cromwell Press, Trowbridge

For the first teachers and students of the
Priest Seminary of the Christian Community, Hamburg

Contents

Introduction: The Virgin Birth

Ever since the Gospels were first written, Christians have been filled with wonder at what they have to tell. The evangelists themselves constantly stress the amazement of those who encountered Jesus, when he spoke with divine 'authority,' when he performed miracles, above all when he rose from the dead. Many of these things are indeed hard to understand, and we shall have to wrestle with questions about several of them as we try to find our way to at least some part of 'what really happened.' The knowledge that they challenged everything familiar and normal from the very beginning, for the earliest Christians, should remind us that the issues they pose are not between old-fashioned credulity and sceptical modernity. Moreover, many have come to the painful realization that the liberalizing of Christian thought in modern times, substituting a Jesus who is a good man and a teacher of morals, a Jesus without the miracles or the overcoming of death, has resulted in something that cannot bear the weight of the Christian claim — cannot continue to hold up the structures of commitment and faith that have made Christianity such a potent force in culture and history. Such a Jesus will become only one voice in an increasingly complex modern world, and perhaps cease to be heard at all. The Church is ill-advised to think it can go on without having strong convictions on such matters as the resurrection or the divine origins of Jesus. The difficulty of finding modern answers to the challenge is formidable. But without the challenge, and the amazement, of the biblical Jesus, we shall never understand what made the early Christians sure that they had experienced a new and direct revelation of the divine. And perhaps nowhere has the wonder been greater, and the quandaries of modern Christianity more striking, than in reading the story (or stories) of Jesus' miraculous birth.

We must be able to share the amazement of the early Christians, but it would be wrong to think that unlike ourselves they approached the story with unthinking faith. Indeed, according to one of the Gospels his mother Mary herself more than wondered at the event and demanded, with some degree of outspokenness considering it was an angel who foretold it to her — 'How can this be, seeing that I know not a man?' (Luke 1:34). If more than a few in modern times have been inclined to repeat that question, including many from within the Church (and not excepting some of its leaders), they are echoing a question in the Gospel itself. And answers were expected. Yet the angel's words came true, as it appears from what follows, and the birth of her child was the miracle we have come to know as the virgin birth.

What did they understand by this event? What really happened? These are the questions we now have to face if Christianity is to make any sense to future generations.

Isaiah's virgin: or was it just a young woman?

Over the generations Christians have meditated upon the meaning of such an extraordinary event. But as often happens when people think about something intensively and over a long time, it does not necessarily become any clearer — rather, unfortunately, the reverse. The evangelist known as Matthew had already thought about the matter deeply even before Luke, for into his version of events he weaves a surprising number of subtle allusions as well as direct quotations from the Scriptures, as he would still have thought of them, in which he purports to recognize among many other things foreshadowings of the idea that the Messiah sent by God to his people Israel would be born of a virgin. Nowadays we are so familiar with this kind of 'foreshadowing' idea, and it has been applied so pervasively to the Scriptures that for Christians they have turned into the 'Old Testament,' having meaning only in this prototypical sense, as pointing to the 'New.' It may even be a slight shock to realize that, to the most learned and pious of that time, this was still a most extraordinary way of looking at the Hebrew sacred books, associated at best with schismatic groups like the Essenes, who had split with the rest of Judaism and gone off into the desert near the Dead Sea. We have a mass of their writings in the Dead Sea Scrolls. Matthew may well have some connection with them. By their friends, they were seen as pioneering new interpretations of the Bible and a new ideal of community-life, with welfare provision and sharing of goods; in the eyes of their detractors, they were a fringe sect who thought that all the Bible had been written specially to point to them.

There are other things we tend to forget too. For example: most of the texts Matthew uses to prove his case for Jesus had never previously been thought to apply to the Messiah at all. Conversely, many of the texts which Jews believe do mean to speak of the Messiah, are ignored in Christian tradition. Most questionable of all is the assumption that the idea of a virgin birth was present in the Bible. But surely, you may say, there is Isaiah's celebrated 'Behold a virgin shall conceive ...' (Isa.7:14)? This looks unambiguous enough, but on close inspection it turns out that there is none but the flimsiest evidence — or wishful thinking — that Jewish prophetic traditions knew anything about a virgin birth, or even that Isaiah really said any such thing as stands in our modern Bibles, (though admittedly it was in the old Greek and Latin translations before it got into ours.)

When we turn to the Hebrew of Isaiah, we soon discover that the word he uses which was rendered 'virgin' in the Greek and Latin Bibles is, in the original Hebrew, 'alma. And 'alma means essentially a young woman who has passed the age of puberty: obviously it might be the case that an 'alma is a virgin (especially in a strict Israelite society). The Greek translator evidently thought it natural, but the word does not carry any connotations of virginity as such, and when it is said that a young woman will bear a son there is no reference to a miracle:

Behold the young woman will be (or: is) with child, and
give birth to a son, and she will call him (lit. call his name)
Emmanu-el.

Isaiah is said to have spoken this oracle to the hostile (in biblical terms, the 'wicked') king Ahaz in the eighth century BC. It
has the air of alluding, like many Old Testament prophecies, to
events that hearers of the prophet would have recognized and
understood. Note that she is 'the young woman' rather than 'a
young woman' — suggesting a definite situation known to his
hearers, and alluding to the already expected Davidic prince that
she will bear. He will be a divinely guided champion whom God
will enable to restore his oppressed people. He will show, Isaiah
intimates, that 'God is with us.' Note too that *she* will name him,
not a vague 'they' as in Matthew's Greek citation. Opinion about
the precise meaning of the oracle has varied. Modern scholarship has suggested that the obvious reference is to the prophet's
own son (so that the definite article in 'the young woman' makes
it somewhat like our colloquial expression 'the wife'). Oftener,
in antiquity, the oracle was thought to have referred to King
Hezekiah, the exemplary Davidic 'good king' of Jewish tradition — and other scholars still endorse this view. One thing is
however clear about the passage. It was never used by the Jewish
tradition to refer to the Messiah.

Furthermore, the whole emphasis on virginity which was so
strong in Christianity with its hermits, monks and nuns and the
cult of the Virgin had no counterpart in Jewish attitudes. God at
the very beginning of the Bible had commanded all creatures to
go forth and multiply, and having children was a prime duty of
Jewish men and women. Once again it is only with those diver-
gent Essenes and the like that we have even a hint of valuing
solitary life or abstinence. Even there abstinence or virginity is
more likely an indication of ritual purity, such as was demanded
of a priest for a specified time before entering the Temple — in
their separate establishment at Qumran the Essenes were perhaps extending the idea of a holy place to include their whole

life-setting. Still, the condition would be temporary and dictated by special (even if extended) circumstances, so to speak, rather than considered important in itself; outside Qumran, Essenes were also known to marry.

But even if there had been a tradition of valuing virginity, and even though there was in the Greek Bible-translation a prophecy of a virgin who would bear a son, it is clear that this is not how Matthew came by his all-important idea. His citation of Isaiah 7:14 is of a piece with all the other passages of scripture he quotes. Virtually every detailed and scholarly study of Matthew's text has tended to produce the same conclusion about these quotations, namely that they are the last and most personal layer in the composition of the Gospel. In content and in their formulaic expression they stand out and are largely unique to Matthew's Gospel. Attempts to derive from the Old Testament passages the basic ideas 'fulfilled' in the Gospel story have failed to convince, whereas it has struck many scholars that they represent the evangelist's own fascination with and discovery of prophetic meaning. The large thematic ideas of redemption and Jesus' mission are not well or even adequately covered by the Old Testament allusions, which only touch strategically on a few of them by way of further 'reflection' at some striking points. It seems undeniable that Matthew has recounted the story he has to tell, and then brought in the quotations to show (he believes) that it was hinted at in the Bible. Isaiah 7:14 is no different, and was probably introduced into the picture by the evangelist. Where he got the idea of referring it to a virgin birth remains unclear.

Matthew undoubtedly knew Hebrew, and while he quotes the Bible in Greek, it is not his authority. Recently in fact a good case has been made that the Gospel was originally composed in Hebrew. But even in the Greek version the evangelist frequently changes the usual Greek Bible-text, the so-called Septuagint, or 'Text of the Seventy (Elders),' in a way that shows knowledge of the original Hebrew version. If he uses the rendering *parthenos* ('virgin'), it is therefore by choice. No-one knows quite why the old Greek translation adopted the reading: but Matthew took it over deliberately, because he wanted to find evidence of Jesus' birth being alluded to in the prophets. He would have known too, however, that the passage did not in any way show that Jesus was the Messiah — rather it would exhibit him as the type of Davidic prince, like good King Hezekiah, who upheld what the Old Testament prophets regarded as the true religion of Israel. He would be God's champion against those 'bad kings' such as Ahaz or more recently King Herod, who oppressed God's people.

Matthew quite evidently regards the virgin birth as overwhelmingly important and a central mystery, as we can see by his inclusion of it prior to the material he shares with the other evangelists, and by his determined effort to find it where no-one had ever found it before. But wherever he found the idea, his point seems to be essentially a theological one, rather than, if I may put it in this way, a story-telling one — an attempt to say what happened at Jesus' birth. That does not mean we need to follow those sceptics who think that Matthew simply made up the whole thing to illustrate his theological views. In fact the infancy material is so different from the rest of the Gospel of Matthew that we must rather assume he received it from the tradition, presumably of the community in which he himself lived, and reworked it himself only slightly. Luke on the other hand is (among other things) a rather good writer, and his well-told story includes the excitement and human drama of the exchange of views between Mary and the angel, so that we as readers wonder how it is going to turn out. But Matthew does not let us linger in expectation and uncertainty, and does not seem much to value the story-teller's art: when Mary is found to be with child, he cuts in immediately to inform us that it was by the Holy Spirit. That, he seems to say, is the important point here. And when he quotes the Scriptures, it does not really invite us to go back to the passage mentioned and explore its setting and ampler signification. He wants us to know that Isaiah pointed to the virgin birth — but from that moment any further interest in Isaiah drops out, since it is the virgin birth itself which is really important. Naturally perhaps for one of the first Christians, all the interest is directed forward to the figure of Jesus.

Yet that is also one reason why Matthew's account is basically different from a genuinely Jewish way of reading the Scriptures, which some have thought he employed, called a *midrash*. What is meant by the term *midrash* ('interpretation') is telling a story which helps explain or interpret a passage in the Bible for later times no longer familiar with customs or events mentioned there, or where there are obscurities and difficulties in the content, or in the text itself. Often quite new material is included, certainly shedding new light on what the Bible says. But the thrust of *midrash* is always to explain and illumine what we find in the Bible, not, of course, to relativize the Bible by claiming to know what really happened, as if one could then evaluate what the Bible had made of it from a standpoint of superior knowledge! Yet that is just what Matthew does, for he now knows what was to happen as the unexpected fulfilment of the prophecies, and his overriding point is that it did happen. The point of the Bible is now to explain that amazing event. Jewish opinion was and has remained the exact reverse. The Bible is in no way considered to be all about the Messiah: when the Messiah comes, they believe, he will make plain all the apparent contradictions in the Scriptures.

Matthew's 'theological' interest is still rather different, however, from the kind of theological interest that we find in the later Christian tradition. As a matter of fact, for the theologians, the virgin birth has always been something of a two-edged sword. One of the great concepts with which Christian theology has to wrestle is the tremendous idea that God became incarnate. Many religions have had the belief that God shows himself through an outstanding human figure such as a prophet, or a charismatic leader, even an *avatar* as in Eastern religion through whom a divinity shines out directly in his teachings and deeds as in the case of Krishna. But in none of these is God himself really affected by his mode of manifestation, whereby he chooses to reveal himself to us. There is nothing in these conceptions of God actually sharing the human condition; nothing of Paul's paradox in Philippians of God giving up Godhead, 'emptying himself,' taking the form of lowly minister to human beings and knowing at first hand what it was like to be human, even to the point of experiencing death — and not just death but a violent, even shameful death, being jeered at as a criminal, the most terrible suffering and rejection.

The pathos and inner meaning of Christianity springs from this really amazing idea of what God was prepared to do out of love for his creatures. And one of the central needs in any Christian account is therefore to hold firm to that Pauline assertion that God did indeed take on in the fullest sense the human condition. Yet, if Christ was born in some peculiar way that does not correspond to the normal human manner of birth at all, it is hard to see how this idea can help establish the central values of Christian faith. Moreover Paul himself, who is of course our earliest Christian writer, apparently knows nothing of it. Later theology tried to modulate its attitude rather carefully, and in many later formulations seems to walk something of a tightrope, suggesting that the virgin birth somehow enabled God to take on physicality while retaining his divine purity. Far from Matthew's central wonder at the great and miraculous event, a verse which we still sing from the well-known Christmas hymn ('O come all ye faithful') presents a somewhat poetically awkward (verging on embarrassing) feeling that, since it is to be a virgin birth, God is just about prepared to go through with the incarnation, even though it evidently still takes some doing:

> Lo he abhors not the virgin's womb

(but more likely the verse will have been de-selected anyway by the well-meaning pastor).

Anxious, no doubt, to prevent the central thrust of the Christian faith from being compromised, some recent scholars have even gone so far as to wonder whether the evangelists themselves really meant to say that Jesus was born of a virgin. There is the obvious point that the cult of the Virgin Mary developed rather later than the epoch of Christian beginnings, and indeed received its full authorization only when Christianity went out to become an imperial religion under the emperor Constantine the Great. Helena, the Empress-Mother and herself a devout Christian, was a powerful figure at the Byzantine court, a valuable route of influence to get the attention of her son, and when Constantine was proclaimed as the exalted Christ's literal substitute (or 'vicar') here on earth, it was inevitable that his Mother's role should be seen as reflecting that of the heavenly Mother, able to intercede with her own Son. Getting the ear of authority through the intercession of highly placed contacts, and especially the Empress-Mother, was standard practice in the world of Byzantine politics, where Christianity finally became a world-power, and it explains a good deal about the cult of the saints and the Madonna. Moreover other currents, such as the veneration of the immensely popular virgin Goddess, the Ephesian Artemis (cf. Acts 19), also appear to have paved the way for her cultus. (Jesus' mother was even transported by legend far from the Holy Land to live and subsequently pass away, supposedly, in Artemis' holy city of Ephesus — though there was already, and still is, a flourishing pilgrimage-site of her 'assumption' in Jerusalem.) Attempting to look back, therefore, without the blinkers of hindsight, the Catholic exegete J.A. Fitzmyer questioned whether Luke had really meant what all the well-primed readers of Christendom had thought he meant. Though Mary is a virgin when the angel comes to see her, he only says that God's holy Spirit will hover over her child and its birth. Are we not rushing to conclusions when we suppose that she was supposed to have remained a virgin all along?

But perhaps a scholarly mind is being over-ingenious. After all, Luke is writing for a very general audience, including many pagan converts as well as those with a Jewish background. He would naturally have wanted to avoid the impression that the begetting of God's Son was an event like the pagan legends of heroes begotten by amorous gods and mortal women. He would therefore want to avoid presenting the Spirit as fathering Jesus in any too literal sense that might offend pious Jewish feelings and lead to misunderstandings among the new ex-pagans. The restrained language of overshadowing and hovering probably is, therefore, an allusion to Jesus' divine origination, standing in place of any conventional fatherhood. Moreover, Luke may be the latest of the evangelists, and it seems increasingly likely that Luke actually knew and used Matthew's Gospel, so that he would perhaps be alluding to a mystery already spoken of and enshrined in the tradition. He evidently does not want to place such stress on it as Matthew does, but without pressing it upon his readers makes clear reference to it as a well-known item of the faith. It may be that he wants to complement Matthew's account with different perspectives.

Indeed it is plain that the miracle of Jesus' birth is a mystery that requires caution and suitable preparation if we are to approach it. Thus it can hardly be accidental that Luke presents Jesus' birth in an elaborate tandem with that of John, later called the Baptizer. In his account there is another angelic proclamation, to Zechariah (or Zacharias) as he ministers in the Jerusalem Temple, since he is of priestly descent. Parallels and contrasts suggest themselves intuitively: this is a revelation to a man, as the other is to a woman; it is a revelation to a priestly family, as that was to a kingly family. The one takes place in the holiest place of Judaism, the other in the obscure and rather despised region of Galilee, which will nevertheless turn out to be so important in the Gospel-story. Even more importantly, the opposition between the two places will take on symbolic dimensions in the Gospel tradition. The wife of Zechariah is also unsuitable as the prospective parent, because she has so far been barren and is now beyond the age considered to be that of child-bearing. She has had a long life together with her husband, whereas Mary is still betrothed and just about to start on her married life. The virginity of Mary is thus placed in symbolic parallel with the equally unlikely old age of Elizabeth, yet both bear sons with crucial parts to play in the coming drama. In the famous scene of their meeting, when the baby turns ('leaps') in Mary's womb, it seems metaphorically that the unborn children already meet too, and so are revealed as connected or even sharing the same divine impetus.

The birth-stories also seem to reverse the role of the figures later on: John will appear as the ascetic who lives in the desert, calling on everyone to 'go out' to be baptized and leave behind their sinful lives, whereas his birth is announced in the sacred centre of the populous city, Jerusalem, the mention of the settled rota of the priests stressing the normality of life — which also can be blest. Jesus' birth is announced in far-off Galilee, yet his destiny will bring him, inexorably, to die in Jerusalem. (All of his ministry for Luke comprises Jesus' deeper 'journey' to Jerusalem). John, according to the Gospel tradition (perhaps unhistorically), will conversely die by being beheaded in Herod's fortress in Galilee.

Thus as we look at the two intertwined stories, it seems that the nature of God's miraculous intervention in bringing about the birth of Jesus is already fully spelled out and defined through elaborate counterpointing, even in these very first chapters of Luke's Gospel. A virgin birth is such an extraordinary case that it might help to understand it in terms of similarities and contrasts, Luke seems to suggest through his literary technique, with one which is much more familiar from the Old Testament. Remember Isaac's wife Rebekah in Genesis (ch.25). She too was barren, but at Isaac's prayer God made her conceive; she too received a direct message from God that her children were to be significant, being 'two nations,' just as Mary is told her son will be great and a saviour of his people; the children in Rebekah's womb 'struggled' — for they were the warring opposites in character, Jacob and Esau, whereas John and Jesus are complementary and creative opposites who greeted each other in the womb. Or there was Sarah, Abraham's wife (ch.21), who again bore a child in old age as the Lord had promised: in typical Old Testament fashion, his name is interpreted by clever word-play in Hebrew — just as Luke makes play with the name Jesus, which in its sounds suggests the word for healing or salvation — 'for he will save his people from their sins.' Though dealing with it more lightly, allusively and imaginatively than Matthew, Luke too believes we can be helped by the Scriptures to grasp the further miracle he describes of Jesus' virgin birth, so apparently alien to the Jewish faith.

Perhaps 'Beware of pagan analogies and be guided by comparing the way that God has brought about the great events of sacred history,' is one of the coded messages involved in that parallel weaving of stories: Luke was certainly living in a community with more of a gentile background. So he alludes to the Old Testament 'miracles.' Many of the things God brought about would never have happened at all if everything followed human standards of expectation. And more than ever was that the case with Jesus. Whatever happened at the virgin birth, an awareness of God's guiding, patterning hand in history is a part of what it was meant to say.* It is in the most recent times, of course, that the deepest reservations have been expressed about the virgin birth, and that from Christian theologians; but they have been, not surprisingly, on quite other grounds. Modern scepticism has been less concerned about the appropriateness of the story than about its plausibility. If Luke thought that setting the virgin birth in the larger context of God's traditional and acknowledged miracles could help point interpretation in the right direction, he would be disappointed by modern scholars who have felt that bringing in more miracles was precisely *not* the way forward. In trying to give the Gospel story contemporary meaning and relevance, expositors have in general drawn less and less upon the Bible's claims about Jesus' miracles, the virgin birth — not to mention the resurrection or the ascension.

Believing in miracles

But let us see whether Luke was so wrong after all. Perhaps we need to put our own attitudes under the spotlight. Luke may have been much of his time in appealing to miracles — but then

---

* Nevertheless, of pagan supernatural analogies more later on!

our characteristic modern scepticism is just as much of its time. Many of those who pride themselves on being rationalists in a rationalistic time, as Blake once remarked, in a monkish age would have been monks. Is there really no way we can manage to meet across the centuries?

Let us take a typical modern case. The novelist A.N. Wilson recently wrote a rather popular 'life of Jesus.' Though it makes no pretensions to scholarly research, and is presented more as a contemporary exercise in examining 'what to make' of the phenomenon of Jesus, it no doubt touches the nerve of many people's thoughts today. He is immediately dismissive of any effort to reach behind the stories of Jesus' miracles, or virgin birth, or ascension. What is the point, he asks, of trying to decide whether Jesus really did or did not ascend into heaven from the Mount of Olives? It is not only the miraculousness which is out of date, but the point that the miracle-story makes is equally outmoded. Even if it could be proved to have happened, such an ascension (we now know) would have propelled Jesus into orbit, not into heaven. Before it would make any sense to decide whether you believe in Jesus' ascension or not, you have to accept an archaic cosmology which saw the sky as a sort of vast dish lying over the entire earth, beyond which lay the realm of God and the angels.* If we no longer suppose that the cosmos is laid out in this crude fashion, the question becomes — and not in the mediaeval sense — immaterial.

In the same way, even if it could be proved that Jesus did fulfil a prophecy by being born of a virgin, 'we now know' that this

---

* His account echoes a highly developed school of thought from the last century, called 'Demythologizing.' Then Rudolf Bultmann and his pupils set out to thresh out the 'myths,' as they saw it (like the dish-shaped sky and a route to heaven), from the real point of Christianity — the proclamation or *kerygma* which is independent of the outdated pictorial language. He himself tried to express the real point of Christianity in terms of existential philosophy. Perhaps he thought that if Jesus had come today, he would have been such a philosopher, possibly a university professor?

could only be a freak parthenogenesis. It would remain a biological oddity (known occasionally, I understand, in frogs).

Reading Wilson's account makes us feel confidently modern,
confirming our distance from primitive ideas, reassuring us that
we possess the true standards of verification, put into our hands
by centuries of progress and science. But now let us look at an
analogy in the sphere of science itself, where there are fewer
taboo themes and reassuring gestures are less necessary to our
self-confidence. Let us take the example of an eighteenth-cen-
tury scientist, Joseph Priestley, who as every schoolboy knows
(and of course schoolgirls too) was the discoverer of oxygen.
Here was a decisive event in the history of analytical chemistry,
which had emerged in the eighteenth century, rather late by the
standards of the Scientific Revolution set by seventeenth-century
cosmology and astronomy — cf. the well-known achievements
of Newton. Chemistry was catching up and becoming a true science. Except that Joseph Priestley had never heard of oxygen.
In his own mind, he was out to pin down something which we,
after our school chemistry-lessons, will laugh out of court for
being as chimerical as a boojum or a snark. He was in pursuit
of phlogiston. Phlogiston is the mythical heat-substance which
many people still believed in at that time, supposed to be present
in warm bodies, and much effort was put into the effort to detect
signs of its presence or absence. It was Lavoisier who changed
the paradigm, as we should say nowadays, and coined the term
oxygen, thinking of it as gas connected with special acid-form-
ing properties (oxy- = sharp, acidic). Priestley remained a devout
adherent of the phlogiston-theory for the rest of his days, and no
doubt regarded his achievement of 'de-phlogisticated air' as actually proving it!

But no one in writing the history of science would follow
the line of A.N. Wilson on Jesus. If one were to do so, it would
be immediately necessary to declare that the whole case of
Priestley is a nonsense from beginning to end, a true hunting
of the snark (which as readers of Lewis Carroll will remember even when found turns out not to be there). For it must be

equally nonsensical trying decide whether Priestley had or had not, as he claimed, achieved a 'de-phlogisticated air,' when we now know that there simply is no such thing as phlogiston.

Yet in this case it is absolutely clear that, even if he chose to describe it in ways which we no longer approve, Priestley had been able to focus attention with scientific exactitude upon purified air in a context that was to be decisive, for instance, in treating breathing-problems as well as in developing scientific chemistry. His approach has the experimental and practical hallmarks of science as well as its empirical attitude. We must admire his acumen and scientific approach, his rigorous method of discovery just as much as if he had adopted the system which we now use, following Lavoisier. Priestley is rightly acknowledged in all those school textbooks. For it is actually modern nonsense to suggest that we are culturally locked inside sealed sets of presuppositions and ideas about the world, which no-one from outside, who describes the world in another way, can penetrate. Historians of science have in fact become increasingly fascinated by the exercise of feeling their way inside earlier ways of looking at things. They have rejected the old notion that we should look back in history for the bits of previous thought that agreed with our way of thinking, call that true and essential while all the rest is superstitious nonsense. This is the approach sometimes called the 'Whig' view of history after the old political party which saw everything in terms of gradual progress towards its own views. Everyone who had held anything like one of their ideas was regarded as 'progressive' and a 'forerunner of modern ...' (whatever it might be). Much was thereby distorted, especially in the history of knowledge. For instance: Paracelsus, the Swiss physician, did not think in a modern scientific way, yet it would be erroneous to lump him in with 'mediaeval superstition,' for he pioneered many of the ideas which did develop into scientific thought, and perhaps would not have developed without him — for instance, treating illness with specific remedies. Moreover, he like Joseph Priestley was a clear, powerful thinker in his own way and not

at all confused, just because he did not know things that had
not yet been discovered yet (surely an unreasonable criterion
to condemn him by if ever there was one!). And, of course,
eminently scientific figures such as Isaac Newton have turned
out not to think in modern ways either, yet they are hardly to
be criticized for lack of scientific rigour and clarity! To feel our
way back into their ways of thinking is also fascinatingly to see
how our own emerged.

And that is the rather different point that I would like to
make — different, that is, from the idea that because we have
changed our ideas it would be nonsense to even enter into a
'myth' like the ascension, or the virgin birth, or phlogiston.
For as soon as we know some science, we can understand (if
through a glass darkly, perhaps) what earlier thinkers were
referring to, and what it was like when they thought in their
own way and arrived at discoveries now familiar to us. The attitude that the 'myth' must be laughed out of court, on the other
hand, is the attitude of someone who does not know anything
about the subject.

Anyone who knows just the basics of oxygen can experience
the fascination of seeing Priestley find his way toward its isola-
tion, seeing him come at it from an unfamiliar starting-point,
gradually coming at a concept which we have long used, and
of course now taken far beyond his understanding. We will
respect his search and understand its highly scientific character.
But if we are armchair critics, we will read about his belief in
phlogiston and conclude that he was engaged in a chimerical
enterprise, only made worse by the fact that he thought that
he had found it. And perhaps we do the same in the religious
sphere. The attitude that religious truth has to be separated from
the nonsense of a dish-shaped heaven and a Jesus blasted into
orbit is the attitude of someone who has no idea of the religious
realities which the Gospel might be trying to describe — and
fails to see our own conceptions in historical perspective just as
much as it fails to understand where the evangelist was, as they
say, 'coming from.'

Matthew, in a very different sphere, appears to be in a similar situation to Priestley. He has apprehended what he realizes to be a great mystery of the religious life, made real and living in Jesus, and he uses the Old Testament to explain it and to formulate its significance, even while having to push the Old Testament beyond what it really could explain.

Rather than dismissing the evangelists because they use pictures from the Old Testament, or from archaic cosmology, we would do better to see whether we can find our way to the phenomena they are trying by whatever means to bring before us. We may then be in a position to recognize that they had, metaphorically speaking, discovered oxygen even though they called it dephlogisticated air.

It is the way that the discovery actually breaks the mould of the old concepts and ideas that helps us understand what was meant by a miracle. It has about it the quality of something that will ultimately make us question and rethink everything we thought of as settled before. The proper biblical term for such miracles is revealing: occasionally they are called *paradoxa* (things beyond the reach of normal thought, or impossible to understand), but normally they are 'signs' (*semeia*). The first 'sign' in the Gospel of Luke is the baby Jesus himself, lying in the manger. 'This will be to you a sign,' says the angel (2:12). When they see him, the shepherds will know that the events of redemption have been set in motion, as shortly afterwards will the aged Shimeon who then can die in peace. But it only becomes a 'sign' when we know the revelation of the angelic host — when we see the fact as part of a higher pattern. Otherwise we would see only the most unimportant thing imaginable, a family and their child not even important enough to get themselves a place to stay. The new framework is as important as the event itself, since it is only thereby that it takes on an amazing new significance. Similarly in science a patch of mould on a spoiled sample, which many would have thrown away, famously becomes Pasteur's discovery of penicillin. The real meaning of a 'miracle' is not the vulgar notion that it performs something contrary to laws of nature, but that it reveals something new about the world and makes us change our thinking. (The true alternative to believing in miracles is to suppose we are in the favoured position of knowing absolutely everything about the world already — a very dubiously scientific proposition.) In fact, one might say that every discovery, like a miracle, has something of the quality of a virgin birth, a dawning of undreamed-of significance.* I am not importing modern subtleties and presuppositions into the Gospels here. The Gospels have a rather developed theoretical stance on this subject, which they put into the mouth of Jesus (Matt.13 and parallels). Jesus teaches the people in 'parables,' as the usual translation goes. They are 'comparisons,' or 'pictures,' i.e. representations which are not the thing itself but which convey what it is in some distinctive medium. The 'Kingdom of heaven' is not something that can be placed before people, but they can be nudged toward the necessary insight into what it means by various means — just as within the old frameworks of science something could be posed as requiring the shift from those frameworks to a new one. But people have a way of wanting to stay with the old frameworks, and (at least in the eyes of those who have discerned a ground-breaking new interpretation) they remain obstinately blind to what they need to see. (Sadly, it is still so in science too: the historian Thomas Kuhn showed that adherents of the major scientific theories have to actually die

---

* Of course I do not suggest that the evangelists were 'scientific' in their approach. It is rather that science has nowadays monopolized our approach to discovery, which used to be looked at in a number of other, notably religious ways. It remains a distinctive feature of science that the business of discovery is treated in a highly systematic way and regarded as being (through experiment) under human control. Earlier times felt that the reaching of new insights was less guided by human reason on its own than brought about by mysterious and unexpected factors, attributed to the gods or to God, and granted to those who were worthy to attain them; the latter thereby accepted also a moral responsibility for what they knew.

out before a new 'paradigm' can establish itself.) Jesus applies to them Isaiah's words:

> That hearing you will hear yet not understand; and seeing, you will not perceive ... For their eyes they have closed, lest they should at any time see with their eyes and hear with their ears, and understand with their heart, and change their point-of-view, and I should save them. (Matt.13:14f)

Jesus means that they should see what is happening, all around them, which he describes as the dawning of God's Kingdom. In science, also, the mentally liberating shift to a new viewpoint is closely tied in with empirical events, experiment, observation. It is certainly possible, however, that a stress on the importance of being able to jump to novel insights could become important in itself — rather as in Zen techniques, which use extreme or apparently irrelevant subject matter, precisely to show that what matters is the mental process, the leap to inner 'enlightenment.' There was at least a strong tendency on the part of some adherents, perhaps with a background in cultic or semi-philosophical Mysteries, to push the 'interpretation'-theory of early Christianity in that direction, losing involvement in the events of Jesus' time and life and using them simply as a springboard to 'insight,' *gnosis.* The *Gospel of Thomas,* for example, though it has not gone quite to the lengths of a fully Gnostic theology, stresses the 'mystery of interpretation' as the central arena of salvation. 'Find the interpretation' is there Jesus' central message (*Gospel of Thomas* 1).

The bringing-about of a new orientation, in which some familiar yet unregarded fact or event can become the 'sign' of a new point-of-view, that transforms everything, is certainly a part of the Gospel message, however, and is shown not least by Matthew in his indication of hitherto unregarded sayings and prophecies in the Scriptures.

All this may be a rather damning indictment of the prevalence in religious-scholarly circles of that notion of demythologizing — of rewriting the Gospel in our own terms — which is demanded so often today. But it will still more significant, I hope, in clarifying the nature of our own exploration into the mystery of the virgin birth. It will reveal its power and its meaning, perhaps, if we are able to apprehend it as a 'sign.' And that means knowing the right framework in which to interpret it — just as for the shepherds an ordinary child with its mother locks into a new framework, becomes an indicator, or sign, that shows a whole new world-order beginning.

Matthew tries to make the amazing event understandable to his readers by referring to scriptural texts in a most creative fashion, suggesting that if we can break free of fixed ways of understanding from the past we might find the most startling and liberating truth; Luke tries to draw analogies that bring out the working of God into human events, like an unexpected birth past the usual time of childbearing that changes the lives of a family and brings wonderment to a community. The virgin birth is similar — yet even more disruptive of our usual expectations, demanding a change in our way of thinking and our standards. Are these things that really make no sense to us today? No doubt the Gospel writers would have used other analogies if they had been writing now. But all the analogies would have no other purpose than to awaken something in us, comparable to a researcher's experience in the laboratory (or just with our chemistry set) when grasping 'oxygen' even if we are still having to use the ladder of 'dephlogisticated air' to get there. The laboratory is our religious life. (Depressingly, the demythologizers usually end up by arguing that the texts of the Bible or other ancient sources elude modern interpretation because we cannot know what they are based on.) What will make sense of the stories and the symbols, however, is a recognition which draws on the immediacies of spiritual life, which enables us to recognize them. We can feel too that they are often in a so much more profound and beautiful form, that we can acknowledge them without feeling the need to limit their value to the way that we would most readily talk today. Indeed, unless we are very foolish, we shall find it enriching and humanizing to appreciate other ways of coming to the same knowledge that has value for us now in a particular form. Of course we have gained in intellectual clarity in the modern world. But we should not close our eyes to the fact that we have lost things too: living in close connection with nature, people's experience of it was deeper and more intimate than we can easily imagine. In the spiritual life, the value of things which they felt as myths and miracles may also have been lost as we moved to the detachment, the 'onlooker' perspective so typical of today. We shall not rediscover it by moving away from all the symbols and stories that the Gospels employ, but by recognizing through an inner process and conviction what it was they were talking about — on the analogy of scientific discovery itself. It will take us more deeply and scientifically into the Gospels, not away from them.

We may be able to offer hope, too, to those who, grown dissatisfied with the rationalized and modernized religion of the critical theologians, stress once more not the original sense of the texts of the Bible, their meaning in their time, but what they can mean for those who respond in faith to them now. The danger is that such spirituality comes adrift from the Bible, and from traditional thinking altogether. It is really a false opposition. For all its high claims, critical text-study comes to a dead end, usually ending by concluding only that the text has come from remote and inaccessible times, that its myths were not ours (the past is another country, as a novelist said). On the other hand, spontaneous-response spirituality puts down few roots and comes and goes. We need to be able to find in ourselves what led the ancient religious seers and writers to express themselves as they did. If that is not possible, they can have no abiding religious significance. We need, perhaps, a sort of evolutionary vision: one that might enable us to recognize the values and truths of religion, while acknowledging the changes of perspective that have occurred in their history, and our own truth as only the latest in a quest that we can respect and value humanly alongside our own. But the goal is of course something other than the quest, or even our own answers — that is why it appears as a miracle.

Those pagan analogies

So how are we to begin? How are we to discover what kind of miraculous reality would make sense of the stories about Jesus' birth?

To find it we must get back as far and as deeply as we can into those accounts of the mystery, those stories of a virgin birth. And maybe we will need to look too at some of those stories that the Gospels were apparently trying to rule out. For just as a scientist's work is understood when we know the prevailing theories he was trying to test or to transcend in some way, so the larger picture will include concepts and ideas that help us understand the language, so to speak, of the Gospels. We must understand a language (or a good deal of it) before we can comprehend a single statement in that language. We may have to look, for instance, at some of those pagan stories of miraculous births. And we may have to look wider than just at notions of a virgin birth: Luke already points the way here, showing that the virginity of Mary was seen as parallel to other manifestations of God in sacred history. Even if he was trying to rule out some ideas of what a miraculous birth meant, we would get to know more of the language by knowing precisely what he had in mind. A language also includes those propositions prefaced by a 'not.'

Although it is hardly ever mentioned, and remains scarcely known in Christian circles, the closest parallel to the Gospel story of the virgin birth that can be found in ancient literature comes not from the Bible but from the lays of ancient Rome. The parallels are indeed remarkable.

Legend recounts that in the days before Rome was founded, king Numitor of Alba Longa was overthrown by his ambitious younger brother, Amulius. Moreover, in order to ensure that his predecessor could not look to any future offspring of his line to avenge him on the usurper and retake the throne, the new king also insisted that Numitor's daughter should never marry. This he ensured by making her a Vestal Virgin. (The reader will probably recall that these priestesses were all dedicated virgins who guarded the sacred fire of Vesta, goddess of home and hearth.) Rhea Silvia, or Ilia as she is sometimes called, became a vestal. Imagine the scandal, then, when she was soon afterwards found to be with child. Despite her claims that she was pure, and that the twins who were born to her were of divine origination, being sons of Mars, Amulius seized the children and had them cast adrift in the River Tiber. They survived, however, since they were found where they came to ground and suckled by a wolf and a woodpecker (both sacred to Mars) under a fig-tree growing on the very site of the future Rome. They grew up under the care of a humble herdsman and his wife, and eventually returned to avenge their father. This done, the two youths, called Romulus and Remus, went on to found a new city, Rome.

A little reflection will soon indicate a plethora of thematic links with the stories we know from the New Testament. Not only is there the obvious theme of the virgin who is found to be with child, but also the scandal caused thereby, even if Matthew plays this down to stress the theology; in the Roman case too the divine origin of the boys resolves the issue and reveals their true greatness. And in the background there is the related theme of the false king versus the true (cf. Herod versus the 'king of the Jews'), and the important motif of the false king's efforts to have the children who threaten his rule done away with (the massacre of the innocents). The escape of the children and their upbringing in humble circumstances is of course a well-known romance theme. But it is clearly not unrelated to the idea of the humble circumstances of the child in the Gospels, who is nevertheless of true Davidic descent and who survives the clutches of the false king Herod by escaping to another place. Jesus too returns to replace the false kingship with true kingship — though in a very different sense from the Roman legend! Nevertheless, scholars have long known and pointed out that the terminology of 'Gospel,' or proclamation of the (good) news, comes fundamentally from the cult of the deified Roman Emperors, the successors in some sense to the status and power of the founder and king of Rome. The Emperor's birthday or the anniversary of his accession day especially was proclaimed as a celebration, and a manifestation of his divine right to rule the Empire. A time of plenty and a new era was said to dawn with his coming.

It is unlikely that the Gospels were drawing directly on the legend of Rome. Nevertheless, we may be sure that many of their first readers felt that their language and motifs were not unfamiliar. Both Matthew and Luke seem to steer us away from too much connection with pagan stories by stressing, in their different ways, the Old Testament. But that too means they were aware of possible interpretations that readers might make. Luke was perhaps naturally a talented writer. But from the formal training behind his style (use of properly phrased dedications, correct language, etc.) he must undoubtedly have had a classical 'general education,' as it used to be called.

Yet it is still rather unlikely that he was drawing directly on a Roman tale. Increasingly there is support for the idea, mentioned already, that he was rather drawing on a knowledge of the Christian tradition which already included Matthew's Gospel, which he wanted to complement and interpret for his own audience. Matthew's Gospel was extraordinarily popular among the early churches, whereas Mark's remained obscure and rarely commented on, and John's 'more spiritual Gospel' was long controversial and associated with heretics. And Matthew is beyond all doubt to be located in a Jewish-Christian community, though with gentile members coming in too: he is not likely to have borrowed a Roman tale.

Nevertheless we need to let these themes echo in our minds. For Matthew associates with the virgin birth the coming of the Magi. Though our Reformation predecessors considered them under the very general category 'wise men,' these Magi were (strictly speaking) a distinctive group well known in antiquity; they were a tribe of fire-worshipping priests who maintained the Zoroastrian faith, the archaic religion of Persia (Iran). They were celebrated for their extraordinary fire-rituals and for their striking prophecies of the end of the world, which were certainly later used by some of the fathers of the Church. The Magi believed in the coming of a 'great King' in the last days, who would be a World-Saviour — a conception that had perhaps grown up from older ideas in the time of the far-flung rule of the Persians. The myths about him draw on the background of kingly legends glimpsed in the story of Romulus, and like him the 'great King' would be born of a virgin. The mighty Empire of the Persians had of course been swallowed up in Alexander's still mightier conquest of the known world, but in the course of time it had scattered these Magi across the Middle East, and there groups of them still remained wherever the Empire and its religion had been. Many of Matthew's readers would have been struck that these notable pagan seers and prophets were represented as expecting the birth of Jesus. So perhaps the pagan connection is a clue after all. His gentile Christian members would no doubt have felt especially heartened and sense that they had been found a role in the story to fulfil as pagans finding their way to Christ.

There are other pagan analogies too. But the Jewish world must somehow be the setting in which we discover how they relate to the Gospels. We need to return to Judaism, with the unlikely addition of a note of romance.

A therapeutic romance

By the time of Jesus, Jews and pagans had long been talking to each other. We have much evidence now from ancient discoveries that Jews had taken an active part in the culture of the ancient world. Despite the fact that they believed in their special destiny, they were in no sense living in a ghetto. Nor were they the xenophobic travesty still sometimes assumed (sadly based on situations under persecution that were real enough, though belonging to a much later time). The Greek-educated Jews of Alexandria were even, around this time, embarking on a widespread campaign to spread Jewish ideas, and considered it possible that all the nations would come to accept the laws of Moses. Judaism had a high profile at Rome, and many philosophers were coming to the view that reality was One (as Plotinus, the great Neoplatonist, would say), so that monotheism was, so to speak, in the air. Likewise the Jews did not reject pagan learning and science, but believed it was a partial expression of the truth that they had been given directly and whole by God in the Scriptures (which sometimes had to be treated very ingeniously and allegorically to prove it).

The sect of Essenes has been mentioned already, in connection with the Dead Sea Scrolls. There were also very similar-sounding groups near Alexandria, such as the Therapeutae: they were Jews who had developed religious ideas to meet this situation, and broken with the still conservative Temple and the main Jewish parties so well known to readers of the Gospel, the Sadducees and the Pharisees. It is most probably from their circles that we have a work which comes from the period of Christian beginnings, and deals with many of the issues we have just discussed under the guise of retelling a biblical story — that of *Joseph and Aseneth.*

Aseneth is the Egyptian princess — or so the story had come to be told — the daughter of Potiphar (Pentephres), whom Pharaoh gave to the patriarch Joseph as his wife (Gen.41). The simple narrative lines of Genesis have been expanded into a romance of considerable length, with a strongly religious emphasis as well as the love interest we should expect of such a work. The treatment is intended to bring out themes of its own age rather than of hoary antiquity. Put briefly, marrying Joseph may seem like one small step for a princess, but her conversion to Judaism is portrayed as a giant leap for paganism. It is her inner transformation from an idolatrous Egyptian into a bride suitable for the pure, holy representative of Judaism that is made to evoke the admiration and awe of the reader. Every step of it is explored psychologically and spiritually, from the moment she sees Joseph and falls desperately in love. Thus she enacts the process of a pagan finding the fulfilment of her instinctive love in one who, in the story, seems almost an embodiment of God himself — indeed Joseph is called 'son of God.'

The implications can best be understood in the light of that theory that paganism would find its way to accepting the laws of Moses and his religious monotheism as the answer to its own search. With this among the Essenes went a remarkable theory which will turn out to be of some importance: the theory of the 'double revelation.' For the Essenes, in line with the general Jewish attitude that everything was to be found in the Bible, believed that Judaism and the Scriptures embodied an esoteric wisdom, which God had graciously made known to those of his people whom he chose as his leaders and prophets. They were chosen (sometimes even from before their birth, like Jacob and Esau), and were made privy to God's designs. But the 'heavenly secrets' on which the secret wisdom was based also reached humankind in another way, through the fallen angels; the apocryphal *Book of Enoch* was used extensively by the Essenes and related groups, and it told the story in detail. Moreover there are certainly refractions of it in the biblical references to Lucifer and his fall from heaven like a shooting-star. According to *Enoch,* the fallen angels had not only rebelled against God, but betrayed the divine secrets which they knew to men — only, however, in fragments and without revealing the whole grand design of God's purposes which would enable humanity to use them rightly. Nevertheless on this foundation the great pagan civilizations had sprung up, from Babel and Egypt to Greece and Rome.

Now this meant that when Jews encountered the culture of the Greek and Roman world they believed that everything in paganism, including all its philosophy, had already been known in its real and original significance by the men of God, such as Moses and the patriarchs, whom they considered the guardians of the deeper wisdom of Judaism. The Essenes who wrote the Dead Sea Scrolls just before the time of Jesus possessed many of their 'revelations,' such as the *Testaments of the Patriarchs,* which were supposed to embody this ancient true wisdom, and they thought that in the 'age to come' it would be made known to the whole world — and perhaps quite soon — though for now its mysteries were their treasured secret. Be that as it may, the effect on the relations between pagan and Jewish religious ideas was profound. For pagan religion could be understood as one fragment of the truth soon to be revealed to humanity — and the key to all the fragments was Judaism, especially in its esoteric deeper side. As a result, pagan and Jewish ideas could come together in a very creative way. For although in its old, 'Luciferic' form the pagan wisdom had been stolen from God and was morally suspect, its content could also be found in a new, forward-looking form that was crucially linked to the apocalyptic vision of the future provided by Judaism.

Our religious romance contains much that makes sense when we understand this. When Aseneth undergoes her religious awakening, it takes the form of an 'initiation' — with apparent allusions to rites which would have reminded pagan readers of the celebrated yet highly obscure secret cults called the Mysteries. Psychologically challenging and even dramatic in nature, these cultic associations offered a deeper religious experience to the chosen few in the ancient world, giving them (as we hear) an assurance of immortality and a direct glimpse of the divine. Beyond that, everything was highly secret as their name suggests, but they had tremendous authority with the ordinary people too. Aseneth's initiation, however, will bring her to a novel religious insight from a pagan point of view — namely to recognize the divine man Joseph, the representative of Judaism. She goes through the agonies of humiliation and repentance, and an all-embracing 'change of mind' in that profound sense of the Mysteries. Her pagan-Jewish religious transformation probably reflects in reality the very rituals of the Therapeutae themselves. Thus we can see how Mystery rites were being introduced into Jewish life, not in a backsliding way, but in the belief that Judaism could fulfil pagan expectations as well as the traditional biblical ones and bring in a new world-revelation. The partial, stolen wisdom of the pagan past would find its true meaning in the divine pattern of the future, which would turn out to be the grand, apocalyptic finale of the biblical story.

It will be obvious that many of these ideas, though they later disappeared again from Judaism, are of the very kind which grew further and are central in Christianity: a new world-revelation growing from Jewish and biblical roots, yet reaching out to the gentiles, the fulfilment of universal history etc. Indeed, until quite recently many scholars still thought that in describing the Therapeutae among whom it originated, the writer Philo of Alexandria must actually have been characterizing the early Christian monks. Now however, since the discovery of the Dead Sea Scrolls, we can be sure that such groups as the Essenes and Therapeutae already existed in pre-Christian times, as representatives of a rather esoteric Judaism.

Now, that is our perspective, looking back. But I have mentioned the curious romance of *Joseph and Aseneth* rather to try and look at it from the perspective of readers of the Gospels in the earliest times, when they were newly written. For there are passages in it which can strike us in their similarity to the scenes from Matthew and Luke. The understanding of the Gospels here has perhaps been held back because scholars looked too narrowly for parallels to the virgin birth — and failed to find them in any form that could connect directly with the Gospels. But if we are looking for the larger context, we need to sample the whole symbolic and religious language, as I expressed it, in which their statements could be meaningfully read. And here the esoteric romance of the Therapeutae offers some extremely interesting clues. It does not speak of a birth, but of a virgin and her coming marriage to a 'royal' Jewish figure: and birth and marriage could both be metaphors for the Mystery-union with the higher world of visionary truth. Matthew's Gospel likewise starts with a virgin about to be married. Yet further metaphors for an encounter with the higher world could be: the meeting with an angel, or the rising of a new star. These too we encounter in connection with Aseneth's initiation.

She has turned to and prayed devoutly to the true God:

> And as Aseneth had finished making confession to the Lord,
> behold the morning star rose out of heaven in the east. And

Aseneth saw it and rejoiced and said: 'So the Lord God
listened to my prayer, because this star rose as a messenger
and herald of the light ...' (*Joseph and Aseneth* 14).

Her intuition of a divine 'messenger' immediately takes on still
stronger conviction, and is deepened into a spiritual experience:

And Aseneth kept looking, and behold, close to the morning star the heaven was parted and a great and unutterable
light appeared. And Aseneth saw it and fell on her face
among the ashes. And a man (i.e. an angel) from heaven
came to her and stood by Aseneth's head. And he called her
and said, 'Aseneth, Aseneth.' And she said, 'Who is he that
calls me ...?'
And the man called her a second time and said,
'Aseneth, Aseneth.' And she said, 'Behold, here I am, Lord.
Who are you, tell me?' And the man said, 'I am chief of the
house of the Lord and commander of the whole host of the
Most High' (i.e. the archangel Michael).

He tells her to rise and to remove her veil: for in an obscure passage following he explains that since she is a pure virgin, she may
stand before God without shame just as might any young man.
We do not need to unravel the difficulties of the text here — only
to note that virginity appears to be a factor of some importance in
this 'annunciation' or initiation scene. Certain scholars have suggested that a symbolism of androgyny is intended, rather after the
manner of the Mysteries. There it symbolized primal wholeness,
and pre-maturation lack of sexual identity prior to being initiated
into the roles of man and woman. At any rate, Aseneth is told that
she has reached the first stage of her transition from paganism
to true religion, and stands under the protection of the heavenly
virgin Repentance:

'For Repentance is in the heavens, an exceedingly beautiful and good daughter of the Most High. And she herself

> entreats the Most High God for you at all times and for all
> who repent in the name of the Most High God ...And she
> herself is guardian of all virgins. ... And because she loves
> you virgins, I love you too.
>
> And Joseph will come to you today, and see you and rejoice
> over you, and love you, and he will be your bridegroom,
> and you will be a bride for him for ever and ever. And now
> listen to me, Aseneth, chaste virgin, and dress in your wed-
> ding robe, the ancient and first robe which is laid up in your
> chamber since eternity ....'

Clearly the wedding robe is symbolic, indicating the primal
glory, perhaps, which we lay aside on earth and in the fallen
world but which can be restored through initiation. But the several elements altogether — the stress on virginity, the impending marriage (to a Joseph), the star-messenger, the annunciation
of her future destiny by the angel from the Most High — bear
more than a casual likeness to the stories in the early chapters of
Matthew and Luke's Gospels.

Another resemblance is the tendency of the central female
figure especially to break into verse. When she turns to the true
God, Aseneth has a long verse apostrophe in which she describes
herself as humbled and despised by all people. She is a virgin and
now calls herself an 'orphan' because her new faith has made her
parents and her own race reject her. Though differently realized,
the theme of rejection by all the world is similar to the plight of
the Holy Family with nowhere to stay; and the poetry itself has
some distinct similarities:

> But I have heard many saying
> that the God of the Hebrews is a true God,
> and a living God, and a merciful God,
> and compassionate and long-suffering and pitiful and
>   gentle
> and does not count the sin of a humble person ....

Maybe he will look upon my humiliation
and have mercy upon me.

Aseneth here is not far removed from the famous song of Mary
(or was it Elizabeth?):

For he has regarded the lowliness of his handmaid,
and behold, henceforth all generations will call me blessed.
Holy is his name,
and his mercy is from generation to generation
on those who fear him.

The fact that the manuscripts of the Gospel of Luke sometimes
assign the *Magnificat* to Mary and sometimes to Elizabeth has
reinforced scholars in their view that the songs in the infancy
chapters are not written by Luke, but are taken over from Jewish
circles close to John the Baptist (Elizabeth is, of course, his
mother) or from Jewish liturgical poetry more generally — even
battle-hymns have been proposed!. They have little direct connection with the situation, do not mention the birth of a child,
but have many links to Hebrew poetry and psalms. Likewise the
poetical passages in *Joseph and Aseneth* have been thought to
come from an already existing background of liturgy, and some
elements of them apparently survive in company with other
Jewish liturgical quotations in the Easter-address, for example, of
the Christian bishop Melito of Sardis. A similar background for
both sets of poetic effusions, somehow growing out of the Jewish
liturgical poetry and prayers in a setting where their point was
heightened through special religious expectations, is therefore
highly plausible.

Altogether, then, the story of Aseneth and her conversion,
together with her marriage to Joseph, has truly remarkable
affinities to the Gospel story of Mary. Some scholars have even
thought that Mary's husband Joseph is supposed to echo the biblical patriarch Joseph — e.g. in his going down into Egypt/flight
into Egypt. Yet the Therapeutic romance is just as plainly not

its source. Though there is a star and an angel, a humble virgin to whom God hearkens and who becomes part of his great plan of salvation, there is no virgin birth, and though Joseph is even announced as 'son of God,' there is no divinely begotten child.

Most accounts of the document therefore note its affinities to Christian ideas and leave it at that: *Joseph and Aseneth* shows some of the developments that led to Christianity. That however, as I remarked, is *our* perspective. It is to miss an important point, even if we have not found a 'source.' For it is in helping to clarify the point of view of the first readers of the Gospels, that it makes an immensely important contribution. It came, probably, out of mystic circles in Judaism connected with Mysteries and the new world-vision, and was circulated in the guise of pious romance expanding on a biblical tale. Such literature thus aimed to become well-known, even though the inner teaching of Essenes and Therapeutae was concealed from outsiders. Anyone reading the Gospels in those first centuries, anyone at least who was in any way associated with some form of Mystery Judaism, so to speak, that encouraged gentiles too to become involved (the so-called 'God-fearers'), would surely have found the atmosphere of the miraculous and many of the motifs — the star, a virgin meeting an angel, the prophecy of great world-transforming events bringing salvation — familiar and immediately suggestive indeed of *Joseph and Aseneth* and doubtless other similar works that have been lost.

They would have supposed that these works we term Gospels were similar productions, hinting at great Mysteries, at an extension of the redemptive hope to all the gentiles though with the Jewish faith as the key to its meaning. Though it has some features of a modern novel, readers would have considered that the story was 'true' because it was in the Bible. At the same time it must have been as obvious to most of them as to us that in *Joseph and Aseneth* the central figures are used to hint at the new rites and teachings, fusing Jewish and gentile ideas, of the mystic sect which produced it. But they would have thought of these as being the deeper meaning of the Bible-story itself, unless they chose to reject them outright. They would have thought too, I suspect, that the Joseph and Mary of the Gospels evidently belonged to some such sect or stood for its representative figures: hoping and trusting that they were the ones destined to bring into the world the child who would realize in historical truth their all-embracing vision of the future. Their miracle-child would be the one who would make a new sense of humankind's religious hopes and overturn the established order, historical and interpretative, based on older readings of the Bible.

As we begin to draw closer to tracking down the sources of the virgin birth idea, we shall find that much in their suppositions will be confirmed.

1. Memoirs of Joseph and Mary?

Ask Joseph and Mary

So stories about an angel and a star, and a new phase of providential world-history unfolding, would certainly have made *some* sense initially to contemporary readers of Matthew and Luke. Yet some readers may object here, and perhaps with reason, that this is only to say that Christianity appeared in a particular setting, under particular historical circumstances. The exact content of the Christian message remains unexplained.

The fact of the matter is that, as yet, we have not succeeded in finding a precise link either from the pagan analogies, or from the Essene-Therapeutic background suggested, to the actual virgin-birth story of the Gospels. We have at most a rough setting within which it might start to become comprehensible, at the meeting point of pagan and Jewish ideas in the new world-wide culture that was developing in the early Christian period. But even the Essenes or Therapeutae have nothing directly to tell us of a virgin birth, which seems to have no immediate prototype in any tradition that could conceivably connect with the origins of the Gospels.

Some researchers have taken advantage of the lack of direct connections to press the claims of another approach altogether. If the idea of a virgin birth was not there in any form that could plausibly link with the Gospels, they say, then we must assume it is reported because — it simply happened! And rather than start with the strange and supernatural elements such as the star and the angel, they remind us that in support of the virgin birth having been an actual occurrence, there is much more obvious evidence for closely related events. There is evidence for example that Herod was known to historians as a child-murderer; or,

the evidence supporting Luke concerning the historical situation caused by the census under Quirinius. Our understanding
of the Christian mystery should be derived, from this point of
view, simply from the things which happened. We have been
mistaken then, it would appear, in seeking for a pre-existing religious concept that has been applied to Jesus. We have seen that
the Old Testament analogies adduced by Matthew are generally
admitted to be secondary to his narrative; parallels like *Joseph
and Aseneth* show the way people thought, but they lack the
all-important motif, the virgin birth itself. We should therefore
ask the obvious question. That is: Where should the evangelists
have found the information about Jesus' birth — surely their first
thought must have been, 'Ask Joseph and Mary'? The story of
Jesus' birth and early life could only have come from his parents,
who must have kept a memoir, or perhaps more likely dictated
their reminiscences to those who later followed Jesus, and these
accounts were subsequently passed down by his disciples to the
Gospel-writers.

Now, the plausibility of such an inference is greatly increased
by such early accounts as we possess which tell how the
Gospels were composed. These even appear to make some
mention of exactly such memorials of those who had known
Jesus — or something not too unlike them. Certainly from classical Greek times onward it was a known practice, in the case
of people who became famous, to put together *memorabilia* of
their life and personality. A case often cited for comparison is
the *Memorabilia of Socrates* by his pupil Xenophon. This was
clearly based upon research conducted among other pupils, and
people who had known the philosopher or remembered something about him, and the results were put together into a book
in the interests of illuminating the man behind the ideas. On the
earliest occasions when we hear of a 'Gospel,' in the sense we
now mean of a presentation of Jesus in narrative form, we find
the term used to characterize it was precisely 'memorials by
the apostles.' The early 'apologist' or defender of Christianity
called Justin Martyr in the second century uses this expression

repeatedly. The implication to some is that the apostles worked just like Xenophon, collecting testimonials and recollections, editing the results into a well-researched book. Surely, then, for the childhood parts, they would have talked to Jesus' parents?

But this line of argument has an unfortunate flaw. For as Helmut Koester recently pointed out, the title *Memorabilia of Socrates* is not used before the late sixteenth century AD — it is only a modern way of referring to the book's contents, not an ancient one. No use from the period before Christianity can be found. Justin could not therefore have meant to say that the apostles worked in this way. In reality, the term 'remembrance' in Christian circles had a very different aura and implication. It referred rather to the oral transmission of words or parables of Jesus, which were retold by early Christian prophets and teachers, in church-gatherings, sometimes in a liturgical or ritual setting — but always in a setting of the proclamation of the Gospel, the message of Christianity. Often the living Christ was felt to be present on such occasions as his words and actions were recreated for their hearers. At the early point in the development of Christian tradition at which Justin stands, it was rather accidental if the content of Jesus' Gospel was written down. The reference to the apostles and 'remembering' signifies that the story was handed on by those who had heard his words from the Lord himself, or from his apostles, in a living recreation of the events. In Luke's tradition, the celebration of the eucharist was itself a 'remembrance' of the mystery, through which the sacrifice of Jesus was ever and anew made real to those who partook of the consecrated elements.

So the notion of carefully collected written memoirs, edited into a final form by the evangelist is, unfortunately, an illusion caused by a confusion of terms, and rather too modern a notion of literary composition. The Gospels certainly did not come into being in this way. Moreover the assertions connected with the 'it-just-happened' theory, which claim to show the historicity of events described in the infancy sections of the Gospels, also soon run into serious difficulties under scrutiny. Treated as history, the narratives of the Gospels about Jesus' early life are hard to see as internally consistent accounts of what just happened. The visit of the Magi, for example, though rich in symbolism as we have already seen, is hard to reconcile with the facts reported in the Gospels themselves, where it is quite evident Jesus' own family and even his own brother James (later very central to the movement) did not accept him in his own lifetime. Jesus will pointedly turn from his literal family to those who, he says, are his true family — those who hear God's word and keep it (Luke 8). How is it conceivable that his family forgot the amazing events of his infancy? And indeed how is it possible that the people in the locality who must have known at least of the visit of the Magi did not later follow him, but joined in with the incredulity toward Jesus as merely the 'carpenter's son' and even said he was out of his mind? Other people who encounter Jesus have apparently never heard that he was born in Bethlehem — whereas surely this at the very least should have been remembered as the starting-point for his claim to be the Messiah (John 7:42)?

Moreover, the version of events in the Matthaean story of the search of the Magi and Herod's attempted intervention is very hard to accept as factual reporting. How is it that when the Magi reach Jerusalem and inquire concerning the traditional oracles concerning the birth-place of the Messianic king, Herod cunningly assists them in finding out that the answer is: Bethlehem. Yet, later, he seems to be dependent on them for finding out where to go, and when they will not help him has to resort to large-scale violence to be sure of wiping out his supposed future rival. Even more perplexing is the fact that having been so concerned for the safety of his rule and ruthless in pursuing Jesus, Herod failed to mention the danger from him to his son, Herod Antipas, who subsequently hears of the now grown-up Jesus but clearly has no idea who he is supposed to be.

The 'just-happened' theory is not yet dispensed with, however, because it is possible to argue, at this very point where the Gospel evidence appears dangerously thin, that we touch after all upon happenings verified elsewhere. Just when the improbabilities and inconsistencies seem to be building up, we come upon pieces of evidence that have every appearance of independence and specific detail that confirm the Gospel-story.

Herod the child-murderer and the census under Quirinius

The early fifth-century pagan writer Macrobius is little-read today, and when he is it is mainly for the fascinating obscurity of his discussions, Neoplatonic and otherwise, loosely occasioned by the Roman festival of *Saturnalia*. He also wrote a commentary on Cicero's philosophical reverie, *The Dream of Scipio*. As a learned pagan he is unlikely to have any interest in vindicating the Christian Gospels. Moreover, the report which concerns us involves not only a reference to King Herod but also — and from this derives its interest in the author's original setting — a witticism attributed to the Emperor Augustus. The anecdote about Augustus we have no reason to suppose inauthentic, so that the content of the report must logically go back to a period more or less contemporary with the events themselves. This too is plausible because Macrobius does indeed draw on many sources from earlier and later times.

The content of the anecdote is this. 'It was heard,' says Macrobius, 'that included in the massacre of boys up to two years old, Herod the king of Jews had ordered his own son to be killed. The Emperor Augustus made the comment' — in Greek, the cultured language of the time — 'that it was better to be Herod's pig (Gk. *hus*) than his son (*huios*).' Clearly the Emperor knew that the Jews would not slaughter a pig, as being an unclean animal, and with a sarcastic play on words he contrasts this fastidiousness with the King's readiness nevertheless to murder children and even his own son. In fact, Herod had no less than three of his own sons put to death. But there unfortunately lies the problem. For the anecdote with the quip from Augustus really refers to the objectionable brutality of Herod in putting to death his own son(s) while claiming to be a pious Jew.

It is much less clear that Augustus knew of anything like a massacre of the innocents at Bethlehem. The setting of the anecdote has been furnished by Macrobius, and since he is writing at a time when Christianity had become well established, it is quite possible he is drawing on the Gospel tradition which agrees in spirit with what he knows of Herod from elsewhere — but he has not necessarily critically evaluated the different sources. Though he is definitely not trying to vindicate the Christians, he might well be drawing together things said about Herod in various quarters to prepare the way for his anecdote. Other supposed confirmations are weaker still. Jewish sources hostile to Herod have furnished evidence to the effect that he put to death 'the young' — but they also mention 'the old,' so that their account is probably no more than a generalized description of Herod's cruelty, irrespective of its object. And given that the barbarism of child-murder shocked writers and historians so much, it even becomes rather problematic than helpful that Josephus and others have mentioned individual instances of Herod's crime but passed over the mass slaughter which the Gospel describes at Bethlehem. It would have caused universal outrage, but a clear reference confirming the event is simply lacking in the evidence we have. Any claim that we have to believe in the virgin birth because it is simply reported as having happened can draw little support from the 'historicity' of the stories surrounding it in Matthew. What the stories really seem to do, in vivid imaginative ways, is contrast the rapaciousness and power-hunger of the earthly ruler, his willingness to commit cowardly and barbaric acts, with the ineffectuality of even such ruthless violence when it comes up against the divinely sent 'true king,' the infant Jesus. Though the child-killer Herod may be historical enough, the story of the true prince providentially saved from persecution and whose time will come is a widespread legendary pattern, here used by Matthew to say something about the situation into which Jesus came and about his divine origins.

Clearly, some events in Jesus' childhood may underlie the infancy chapters in Matthew, just as the power-hunger of Herod has a basis in his historical character; but they have developed under the pressure of other, symbolic and theological meanings. That does not mean that they are merely fanciful. If we understood precisely what the factors affecting their development were, we would doubtless see how we are supposed to interpret them — while to those outside .... We shall see that these factors may indeed have followed strict laws of their own, and meant something definite and unambiguous to those in the know. But we have yet to examine the much more copious evidence furnished for historical reality by the Gospel of Luke.

Luke appears to move us on to much more solid ground. He has taken care to establish the framework of his story by relatively detailed references to the political situation prevailing at the time of Jesus' birth. He has indicated the period of the rule of Herod as the time of John's conception; he has mentioned the decree of Augustus requiring a tax-census of 'the whole world,' i.e. the Roman Empire, as the background to the return of Joseph with Mary to Bethlehem; and he has mentioned a well-known governor of Syria as the authority delegated to conduct the census itself. Everyone agrees that Luke is a 'theologian of history,' and the care with which he has set up his story in historical terms once again invites us to treat the other parts of it — relating to the events of Jesus' virginal conception and birth — on the same level. Theology there may be, but Luke himself seems to insist in the strongest possible terms that it is grounded in undeniable historical events.

Luke agrees with Matthew that the beginnings of the story lie in the reign of Herod, called 'Herod the Great' though he was no more than a 'client-king' of Rome, wholly dependent upon the favour of Augustus for his continuing prosperity. The Romans much preferred to rule through local dynasties, rather than having to maintain a full military presence of their own in every province — leaving the legions free to be deployed in border territories where the Empire needed to be held against incursions, repelling anything from bandits in the hills to invasions from the powerful Parthian Empire in the East. Only when things went wrong did they impose 'direct rule' to take control of a province, as happened in the case of Judaea after Herod's death.

Herod managed to maintain his favour with Augustus (despite a moment of tension around 8 BC when the Emperor threatened to withdraw his 'friendship') and, on the whole, to please the Jews. That was remarkable, not least because he was not a real Jew at all but an Idumaean (from the biblical Edom to the south of Judaea), making it quite amazing, perhaps, that he was able to persuade the Jewish authorities to rebuild the Temple more or less in its entirety to suit his designs (and of course with his wealth). The result was spectacular, and he was remembered with gratitude for increasing the prestige and grandeur of the Temple by generations afterward. In Jerusalem indeed, Herod paid punctilious attention to the requirements of Jewish law, though among his more pagan subjects he also made use of the iconography and trappings of pagan kingship. He was, as we have already seen, ruthless in retaining his grip on power.

The Emperor Augustus is almost too well-known a figure to require comment. His long reign — more than forty years — marks the emergence of the Roman Empire out of the chaotic phase of the Civil Wars which ravaged the late Republic and depleted much of the Mediterranean world that was drawn into the struggle. The packed events of that time included the assassination of Julius Caesar, the career of Pompey the Great, the brilliant union and subsequent suicides of Queen Cleopatra of Egypt and Mark Antony, Julius Caesar's follower and would-be successor, and finally the rise of Julius Caesar's adopted son Octavian to a position of sole power and incredible wealth. Calling himself 'son of the deified Caesar' (*divi filius*), the victorious Octavian took the quasi-divine title Augustus, and ruled over the united Roman *imperium* through his personal charisma and unquestioned authority. After the hatred and factions of the Civil Wars, people remembered his restoration of universal peace as a miraculous act, later becoming part of Christian mythology too, which liked the idea that Christ came into a world suddenly and phenomenally at peace with itself.

After the Civil Wars, there was a need for reconstruction, and this meant in the first instance a thorough-going re-assessment and implementation of the imperial taxes. It would be wrong to think, however, of a new and crippling burden. Under the rule of the Roman Senate in the time of the Republic, governors of the provinces had often abused their position to make vast personal fortunes. The provincial population had small chance of redress, since the Senate was the court at which a case against the governor had to be brought, and it showed a sadly unsurprising willingness to decide in favour of its own appointees. (Only occasionally was it possible to get a Cicero as prosecuting lawyer in the case.) The new system was fundamentally fairer, in part because so much of the wealth of the provinces having been plundered, Augustus wanted to build his unified Empire up to greatness by good management and gradual increase of the revenues, rather than risk prompting universal discontentment and immediate rebellion. Basically, the Empire's finances needed putting in order. Among his first acts, therefore, we find the commissioning of 'a general census of property owned in the provinces' (Rostovtzeff). The census did not take place everywhere all at once; nevertheless the call for this general assessment is probably what we should understand from Luke's reference to Augustus' decree ordering a 'tax-census of the entire (Roman) world.'

Also well-known to history is the governor, or, to give him his proper title, legate of Syria, Publius Sulpicius Quirinius — though he hardly cuts the same dash as Augustus. English readers may know him as Cyrenius from the King James Version — a curious form which owes its existence to the accident that the Greeks' alphabet contains no 'Q,' so that they had to approximate the spelling of his Latin name as best they could.

The governorship of Syria was an important appointment. Syria had been one of the three superpowers of the old Hellenistic world, and was absolutely crucial to the security of the Roman Empire in the East, where it fronted on to the territories of the Parthians.

Quirinius was given the post after a long career in high office. Tacitus confirms that he had been elected a consul as far back as 12 BC, and we know that he was in charge of extensive military operations in the Middle East some time before 6 BC. Around 4 BC we hear of him as an imperial advisor in Syria, but it was still ten years before he gained his promotion to be official legate in AD 6. The historian Josephus confirms [*Antiquities* XVIII:1,1] that he conducted a census of his new territories, which by then would have loosely included the new Roman Province of Judaea, established when Herod's sons such as Archelaus proved unable to conduct their affairs to Rome's satisfaction. The census of AD 6 was undertaken, says the modern historian Michael Grant, 'in order to make an assessment of the property of the Jews and to liquidate the estate of Archelaus.'

All the elements in Luke's story thus make perfect sense taken individually. But a many-headed hyrda of problem arises when we try to put them together. The reader will recall that John the Baptist is said to have been born under Herod the Great, a little ahead of the birth of Mary's child Jesus — which is the same time-frame that is indicated by Matthew for the events he described. But conventional wisdom holds that Herod died in 4 BC; it will be seen therefore that a full ten years separate the period of these occurrences from the appointment of Quirinius as imperial legate in AD 6. If Joseph and Mary told the evangelists or their research-assistants that they had been caught up in the events of Quirinius' census *and* that they had been persecuted under Herod the Great, their memories must have been exceedingly confused.

Solutions the most sweeping and most tortuous have been sought for these apparent and disturbing contradictions. Almost every element in the picture has been put on a sliding scale to accommodate a theory one way or another. Most scholars believe that the dating under Herod is a bedrock of the tradition, and that the (much later) Christian estimate of Jesus' year of birth, constituting year 1 of our era, is too late. He must actually have been born, they conclude, several years earlier. (It is the final straw, for some, that Jesus was born 'BC'). Desperate assertions have also been made (on no evidence except some gaps in our knowledge that could thereby happily be filled) concerning an earlier legateship supposedly held by Quirinius, around the period needed if he is to coincide with Jesus' redated birth. But this is pure invention, and anyway does not resolve the underlying issue: if Jesus was born under Herod the Great, Judaea would still have been an 'independent' client-kingdom and there simply can be no question of a tax-survey conducted directly by the Romans.

On the other hand, we could move Jesus' birth as the account in Luke suggests to the period of Quirinius' legateship. But that does not solve anything either, because although Quirinius' territory included the recently annexed Province of Judaea, the Province was not identical with the domains of Herod's old kingdom. This meant that, among other things, Galilee was separated off as a 'tetrarchy' still governed by Herod's son Antipas, as yet tenuously in favour with Rome. Now Jesus' family, by all accounts, was living in Galilee. It is a matter of great perplexity, therefore, to see how Quirinius' census could have affected Galileans in the first place, and downright impossible to see how it could have required them actually to cross administrative and political boundaries in order to register an ancestral connection. Finally and conclusively, the Roman authorities were interested exclusively in property and assets, whereas it is evident that Luke's Joseph and Mary have nowhere to stay in Bethlehem, and could not have been subject to a registration of taxable property there.

Drastic rearrangements of the chronology, moving Jesus' date of birth backwards and forwards across ten to fifteen years, therefore do little or nothing to help the situation. There is, however, a slighter adjustment of the conventional view, for which there is considerable evidence and which may just provide the key to the whole complicated affair. For it is possible that Herod the Great did not, after all, end his reign in 4 BC.

Herod's demise was attended by portents in the heavens: an eclipse of the moon shortly and ominously before Passover. But 4 BC is not the only year when we have records of such things — and indeed the eclipse was rather a long time, almost a month, before the Passover in question, casting some doubt on its appropriateness to the case. W.E. Filmer put forward an extremely good argument, on this and a number of other grounds, for 1 BC as the true date of Herod the Great's death; and the possibility has more recently been vindicated by Ormond Edwards, who has solved a number of the remaining problems in the interpretation. We must remember that the ancient world did not have a comprehensive shared calendar or use a single 'era' from which to number the years. Usually a local monarchy numbered the years of its reign from the latest accession, so that to correlate historical information it was necessary to know that the first year of one country's monarch was the tenth year of another's reign, etc. The era of Alexander the Great was referred to for longer historical estimates; the Romans counted their history 'from the founding of the City' — A.U.C., or *ab urbe condita.* So it is not surprising that the co-ordination of ancient history often presents difficulties, or that other reconstructions are conceivable.

To simplify Ormond Edward's argument a little, he believes that if Herod died in 1 BC, something much closer to the traditional date for the birth of Jesus becomes possible. Jesus may have been born, albeit only just, 'in the days of Herod the king' as both Matthew and Luke affirm. (There is no year '0,' so the first full year of Jesus' life would be AD 1). He has made the brilliant suggestion that it is the events following the death of Herod the Great which furnish the real explanation of the Lukan story about the census. On Herod's death, there would have been a survey of his estate, i.e. of the Kingdom of Judaea and its resources, in order to settle his will. The census was in this sense a Jewish affair, conducted within the framework of the existing Herodian Jewish state. It is only there that we can understand the use of tribal and regional criteria which could have demanded the return of persons to their official 'homeland.' The Bible relates how after the conquest of the promised land, each of the twelve tribes was allotted a precise territory. The Romans sometimes required temporary residents in another area to return to their property for registration (so-called home-, or in Greek *kat' oikian* registration). But the concern with ancestry and tribal allocations can only be Jewish in nature. However, we do know that the Romans and even Augustus himself took a keen interest in the fine detail of events after Herod's death. The end of his reign had been troubled. An oath of allegiance to the emperor had raised scruples among the religious, and may have led to 'Zealot' groups rousing rebellion. Augustus almost certainly intervened personally to change the conditions of Herod's will — presumably basing himself upon a shrewd Roman assessment of the situation in Palestine. He denied the Kingdom to Herod's son Archelaus, to whom he had left it, with two of his other sons holding smaller tetrarchies under his overall rule. Instead, Augustus made the tetrarchies independent of Archelaus, the rest of whose kingdom thus became just another petty princedom (technically an 'ethnarchy') itself. Several of the powerful coastal cities were made independent, and the Greek colonies were assigned to Syria. Augustus evidently feared the concentration of power in a region that was showing signs of disloyalty, and his division crippled the resources available to any one of the princes — who in Herodian style were unlikely to co-operate among themselves.

The assessment of the situation must have been made by Augustus' advisors, though it is impossible at this distance in time to know precisely what was said and by whom. There is, however, the odd phrase used by Luke: 'This was the first census under Quirinius ...' Again, many theories have been launched on the shaky foundations of a brief linguistic peculiarity. It has been supposed that there must therefore have been regular censuses throughout the period of Roman involvement in Judaea — but for that there is no actual evidence. In fact, everything that Josephus says about the event of AD 6 stresses Jewish resentment and outrage, which hardly suggests that it was a customary happening. We actually know only of the one Roman census at the time in question. Yet we must take into account, at the same time, that Luke was writing to an audience of the more educated, affecting a good style and formal features such as the dedication to Theophilus. He would not, therefore, unless he himself was very badly informed, have included in his work statements that his readership would soon have discovered to be erroneous. Quirinius was already acting as imperial advisor on Syria around 4 BC. Did he play a part, on behalf of the Emperor, in the testamentary assessment of Herod's kingdom that was remembered afterwards, several years before his official census of his own territories? We simply do not know. But it would be unwise to assume that Luke could have used the phrase 'first census' unless he knew more than we, at this distance in time, are in a position to contradict. It would therefore be unwise, too, to assume that the setting of Luke's Gospel in the history of the period is necessarily shaky and unreliable. Despite a somewhat fuzzy picture (and Luke is, after all, not setting out to write the political history of the age *per se*), the framework of events he describes may well, after all, have a cast-iron basis in historical reality.

That being said, however, it is just as clear that the historical actuality of the time is not the foreground of Luke's narrative. Very much in the same vein as Matthew, who used the rapacity, child-murder and power-seeking of the historical Herod as a foil to his divinely ordained Davidic prince, so, it seems, Luke shapes a narrative that takes elements of history as suggestive features in a richly imagined symbolic tapestry, full of prophecy and poetry and telling parallelisms between Jesus and John, between their births and events in the Old Testament. His contrast is not now between the false king and the true, as in Matthew, so much as between the imperial foreign powers who appear to be in control both over the world and over the chosen people, in defiance of Israel's promised destiny, and the religious hopes, centred in the Temple and the priesthood, of those who stay true to the promises and, like Shimeon, like Zechariah, like Mary, live to see them fulfilled.

A question of ancestry

The return of Joseph to his Davidic homeland makes sense, as we have seen, only in a Jewish — not a Roman — setting. Despite my remarks about Roman fears over developments in the region, make no mistake: the Romans were not in the slightest degree frightened of a king of the Jews. Herod indeed might have had some reason to fear a popular rival, since the loyalties of the people were hard for him to retain for many reasons. But a realistic view of the Roman *imperium* left no room for doubt in any sane person that to struggle against it would be absolutely useless. When the Jews did later revolt they were violently suppressed, the Temple was destroyed, and after the second revolt Jerusalem was destroyed and replaced in AD 135 by the pagan city of Aelia Capitolina, all Jews being banned from its precincts. The Romans were not worried that a king might seize regional power from them. They were worried about regional instability — because they knew that the mighty Parthian Empire in the East would seize any opportunity to make incursions while Rome was occupied with internal difficulties and disturbance. There is no evidence that they took any notice of royal pretenders such as the Davidic dynasty, whose future restoration was anyway, from their point of view if they even knew about it, a mere myth. If Jesus was later punished for making himself 'king of the Jews' it was as a criminal and a threat to public order, not as a rival to Caesar.

There may have been popular support among Jewish religionists, however, for a nationalistic dream of restoring the Davidic line, to which God had promised 'everlasting' reign. Recently there have been interesting re-examinations of the importance given to Jesus' family, most notably his brother James, in pre-orthodox Christianity. Even Paul, who has little to say about the earthly life of Jesus, 'the Messiah according to the flesh,' does not hesitate to affirm that he was born 'of the seed of David.' On the other hand, it appears that Jesus himself either sought to play down his role as Davidic Messiah, in favour of more spiritual ideas than a restored earthly kingdom, or used the conception to challenge his interlocuters over the real significance of the Messianic hope. Our investigations so far have not supported the idea that the Gospel writers were able, or interested, in giving a strictly historical account of the circumstances surrounding the 'virgin birth.' Nevertheless, they again bring forward very precise documentation based on the idea, important for Jewish perspectives, that Jesus was a Davidid, that is, of the line of David.

The paradox inherent in a virgin birth that is nevertheless used to confirm a line of human descent is one that now, therefore, demands our attention. Both Matthew and Luke offer extensive genealogical tables of Jesus' ancestry. Let us leave aside for the moment the well-known fact that there is little in common between them. For both of them conclude with Joseph — and surely this more than anything else is a curious fact considering that both evangelists have insisted upon the miracle of a virgin birth?

Genealogies are a sort of parlour-game nowadays, except that no-one does them in the parlour any more. Researching one's genealogy is for large numbers of people a fascinating exercise in assuaging their curiosity. It is extremely interesting to find out who contributed to one's family-tree, associated often with a certain nostalgic sense of past times. Strangely enough, although we have been taught to believe in the great importance of genetics (sometimes quite erroneously presumed to account for everything about us), the game of family-trees draws its modern charm from the fact that in our society we are not defined by our ancestry. It is harmlessly fascinating because nothing much rests on it. We do not owe our job, or our social prestige, or our self-respect, except in exceedingly rare cases, to our genealogy. And of the genetic aspect one might even say that it remains 'mere biology.' If it is ever possible to recognize family characteristics already appearing far back, it is no more than amusing to notice them (if it is not total wishful thinking) reappearing in parents or siblings.

In the ancient world, all of this was reversed. There was no 'mere biology,' because of course there was no biology at all in the modern sense. The role of father and mother was undoubtedly understood in its basics, but even among educated people in ancient times it was never supposed that the child born to them was the mere product of impersonal genetic forces at work.

Father and mother there must be, but a child was a gift of God, beyond the mere sum of human actions. Furthermore, no characteristic of personality or family make-up was regarded in the parlour-game way, as a neutral feature to be noted as a curiosity when it recurred. No-one could be excused because a character-trait 'ran in the family.' The ancient attitude was much more holistic, one might say, and the value of the person rested upon everything taken together. The sins of the father were thus indeed part of the moral situation of later generations, and this biblical attitude was only gradually tempered by the emergence of a more individualistic morality.

The issue, one must say, was essentially one of acceptance. The child given by God must be accepted by its human parents, and might reveal much about themselves as well. A difficult, disruptive or challenging child might be a judgment from God, but would be accepted as a meaningful moral lesson. A gifted one might be seen as divinely favoured. On the other hand, if a husband thought that his wife had sinned in adultery, he might refuse to accept the child — but the 'biological' question in those days long before DNA could not even have been intelligibly raised. It was often believed that the features of the child depended on the image in its mother's mind of her true husband — or her sinful lover, giving her away. The basis of genealogy was therefore the father's acceptance of the baby as his. (This may sound one-sided, but of course the mother's role was not in doubt as she had just physically produced the child! What needed to be confirmed was the father's acceptance of his paternity.)

The basis of genealogy was thus — acceptance, conferring legitimacy. And strange biblical practices such as substitute paternity (marrying a dead brother's wife to 'raise seed' for him, etc.) make perfect sense when we understand this. And Joseph's acceptance of Jesus' birth in the genealogical sense tells us nothing about 'biological' paternity. It says that he accepted him as a gift of God to a married couple, absolving Mary of any sin that her unexpected pregnancy might, perhaps particularly in Joseph, have suggested.

Much more depended, however, on being properly constituted as a socially legitimate person than in our own highly individualistic society. The other side of the equation was society's acceptance of the child — and here the difference from our own society worked rather the other way. For if on the one hand you were 'lumped in' with your forebears and had to stand for what they made of you, you were also under much less pressure in ancient society than in ours to 'prove yourself,' or show that you could make yourself more than you already were. Being closer to family in its structures, society also took you 'as you were' much as a modern family still tends to do.

Genealogy was thus extremely important, spanning such diverse issues of the fundamental trust between marital partners, the acceptance of God's will, and above all society's recognition of a valid person, whose special place and contribution could be definitively expressed through a family tree of those characteristics — albeit in a way not conceived biologically so much as spiritually. It should not be very surprising, in that light, to discover that a genealogy was not the sort of thing that accrued gradually in a parish register or record office. We cannot suppose that either of the Gospel-genealogies were already in existence down to Joseph, and that Jesus' name was filled in on a dotted line at the end. (For that matter, neither Abraham, nor, in Luke's case, Adam, started off the blank page!) And it should not surprise us either that a person might have different genealogies constructed for different purposes, showing a suitability for particular roles — something we know was in fact the case for certain individuals. For instance, in the enumeration of the tribal dynasties used in the Bible (such as Gen.10) to explain the relationship of Israel to the surrounding nations, the various ethnic groups are sometimes listed in more than one way: so that Seba (Ethiopia), for instance, is both Hamitic and Semitic, Asshur (Assyria) both Semitic and Japhetic. To us this sounds dishonest, but it was almost certainly not so. To understand this we might think, say, of a modern child who shows an aptitude for writing. Neither father nor mother ever published a page, and it turns out (let us say just hypothetically), that it is only when we look back into lateral branches of the families concerned that we discover there has been an evident literary talent, appearing waywardly down the generations. If we ignore for the moment our own interest in the genetics of the case, it is obvious that we could present the links to those talented individuals as, in a special sense, the relevant genealogy of the budding author in the family.

It is clear when we look at it closely that the Matthaean genealogy, first of all, has been constructed for the special purpose of helping us understand Jesus. As an historical record it is open to all sorts of criticism — as, for instance, that Matthew has compressed the list of kings in several places, e.g. so as to omit about fifty years and several reigns after Jehoram (died *c.* 842 BC, whereas Uzziah/Azariah did not commence his reign until about 783). He needs to shorten this section of the genealogy to bring out a pattern he believes is revealed in the descent of the Messiah, with forty-one names for the historical period where Luke over the same stretch has fifty-six. Having shortened the earlier part, he needs to lengthen the later part to make it equivalent in rhythm and actually has to count Jeconiah twice, as the end-term in the monarchical list and as the first term in the post-Exilic list (Matt.1:11f).

Without doubt Matthew believed that the genealogy he offered represented a reality behind the descent and birth of Jesus that transcended the mere listing of chronology. He has found a pattern, and he sees history approximating to that pattern. Neither Matthew nor Luke, in fact, agree with the Bible on the listing of the historical kings or patriarchs. The material in the Gospels is much more like what we find in the Essene work called the 'Little Genesis' or *Book of Jubilees,* which finds a pattern of jubilee-periods (7 times 7 years) running through sacred history. Matthew finds a comparable rhythm of 2 times 7 in the sequence of generations. Jesus' birth, in other words, is not catalogued as another event which just happened, another name added to the genealogical list: it is presented as the clinching insertion of the last piece into a jigsaw puzzle so that the whole picture of God's purposes in history stands revealed. It is Jesus who makes sense of history — not the other way around.

We may not be able to see as yet very clearly into the determining factors behind this vision of rhythmic phases in the unfolding of God's will as Matthew understood it; we may partly be able to do so later. But the thrust of Matthew's presentation is obvious and powerful once we look at it in this way. Once again the fourteenth step has been reached, the last in the whole sequence of the three great ages of history. The last age was the Exile, when the Chosen People were estranged from their promised land, their plight so movingly expressed by the prophet who sat down by the waters of Babylon and wept, and estranged spiritually from their God in punishment for their sins. So now the Exile must be over: with Jesus the restoration is beginning, the sins of Israel are forgiven, and he must be the Messiah, the true Davidic king who will restore God's people. Read in this way, the genealogy has almost apocalyptic force! 'From Abraham to David were fourteen generations, and from David to the Babylonian Exile fourteen more generations; and finally there were fourteen more generations, from the Babylonian Exile to the Messiah' (Matt.1:17).

Luke's genealogy is also based on a significant underlying idea, and it may also be based on significant numbers. 'Although Luke does not specify that his genealogy follows a system of numerical organization,' points out Raymond E. Brown, 'there are many features in the genealogy that support the thesis of a pattern of 7s: e.g. there are seven patriarchs from Adam to Enoch, and then seventy names between Enoch and Jesus, perhaps reflecting the tradition (see *Enoch* 10:12) that there would be seventy generations ... until the judgment.'[*]

The *Book of Enoch* (*1 Enoch*) was again written by the Essenes or their immediate predecessors, and shows that we are once more in the domain of deeper meanings behind the mere events of history. Again, we may not immediately see why they considered the pattern meaningful, but the attitude we need to adopt is

---

[*] Brown, *The Birth of the Messiah*, p.91.

surely to make the attempt, so as to understand what the Gospel-writers in turn meant to say about the coming of Jesus. At any rate, it is evident that a deeper meaning is there, making sense of history rather than the reverse, just as in Matthew. The deeper meaning in this case is not the Messianic kingdom, however, but the revelation of God's Son. The genealogy follows after the Lukan account of the baptism, when Jesus is called God's Son for the first time in the Gospel. Since he is not writing so much for a Jewish audience as Matthew, Luke's concern is to show the universal work of salvation. His genealogy shows that Jesus is like a new 'Adam, son of God' — perhaps echoing Paul's idea of Christ as the 'new Adam' replacing the old, sinful Adam which is otherwise our common inheritance from humanity's past.

In line with his interest in the priestly and prophetic ministry and the promises of religious restoration, rather than Davidic kingship, Luke traces Jesus' qualities through the line of Nathan rather than the royal descent through Solomon which Matthew preferred. In fact, rather than carping over details (often misunderstanding the point of the genealogies altogether), it is important to grasp that it is at this precise point we touch on the basic difference between Matthew and Luke's presentation of Jesus' descent. Rather than the 'critical' theologians, it is Rudolf Steiner who touched on the essential point here, indicating that the two evangelists are concerned with fundamentally different spiritual qualities, not only in the genealogies but in their whole vision of Jesus and what he meant. One of them has regarded Jesus especially as the embodiment of the royal promise made to the line of David: 'Of your kingdom shall be no end;' the other has looked at the priestly and prophetic heritage of Israel. Certainly the resulting figures may increasingly look like two different persons. But biblical genealogies allow for perspectives more flexible and various, as we have seen, than modern genealogies. Maybe Jesus is in some sense two different figures in one. If Essene ideas do lie close behind the patternings of history we find in the Gospels, we should remember that the Essenes who wrote the Dead Sea Scrolls and the *Testaments of the Patriarchs,* in the time just before Christian origins, expected two different Messiahs: a royal Messiah and a priestly one, or even, in other contexts, a composite Messiah who would be both-in-one. Their priestly Messiah in particular looks forward to the Christian religious conception of the role, whereas in Judaism the royal or Davidic Messiah was at bottom always a nationalistic figure. The evangelists probably knew these ideas. Luke probably also knew Matthew's Gospel, but he is unlikely to be offering his own as a corrective. More probably, he is adding a further dimension that will bring out the universalism of the Christian message already foreshadowed by the Essenes and their like, the fulfilment of Jewish destiny but also the greater world's hopes as well. We are back to the vision which we started to unfold in our Introduction, which detected symbolic resonance with the world of special visionary sects behind the stories of the Gospels. The attempts we have studied to replace that suggested avenue with a more literal or factual approach have ended up by rather confirming it. Our results thus come together with the considerations that have occupied us in our first search for a solution.

Before we leave the 'it just happened' scenario, we may touch on one last version of it: a last ditch attempt to resolve all the differences between the two genealogies, and to ascribe them both directly to the parents of Jesus. A once popular traditionalist solution is that Matthew represents the family-tree of Joseph, while that in Luke is the family-tree of Mary. Moreover, the proponents of the theory assert, the effect of this particular solution helps explain the point of the genealogies altogether, since it indicates that Mary too was descended from David. Thus Jesus is both legally-formally a royal child through his acceptance by Joseph, and biologically through his (miraculous) birth from Mary, herself now revealed as a Davidid. It would also explain why in Matthew's narratives of the infancy, all the stress seems to be on Joseph, who gets messages from the angel, is told to flee into Egypt, etc., while in Luke it is Mary who is often centre-stage, and who solemnly treasures the experiences she has had in her heart. It would explain the differences in perspective, and the different features of the infancy stories, such as the Magi *versus* the shepherds, the persecution by Herod *versus* the Roman census. All this makes sense through the simple revelation that the writer of Matthew's Gospel (or his sources) asked Joseph what he remembered, and the author of Luke (or his sources) asked Mary.

Now, quite apart from the fact that it is unheard-of in Jewish society to trace descent through the mother rather than the father, the theory suffers from great difficulties. It seems to meet the needs of later times, when the Jewish concept of descent was no longer understood properly, and reflects a need to shore up the Davidic lineage of Jesus by bringing Mary in. In fact, it can be traced back no earlier than the late Middle Ages (*c.* 1500). But even if one could accept that Mary had somehow forgotten about the Magi, not to mention the Flight into Egypt, and that Joseph had failed to recall the difficulties caused by the census or the visit of the shepherds — one would have to assume not just that their memories were both oddly selective, but, more damagingly, that after the events they never talked to each other about them! Only in that way could one possibly explain how they elaborated such totally diverse accounts.

It is a standard theological students' joke that this does not sound like the sort of good relationship we must hope was the setting for Jesus' early life. In a very strange and not at all literal way, however, a marital crisis concerning a most unexpected baby will turn out to offer a lead to the deeper meaning of several of these very scenes. We must turn to a story that apparently has nothing to do with Jesus, because it takes us back to the times of Noah and the Flood. And to investigate what it means we must turn to another chapter.

2. The Shocking Truth

A scandalous birth

We come upon a story that may help further in understanding what the evangelists have to say to us, if we turn to a document discovered among the Dead Sea Scrolls. The ever-growing collection of the Scrolls, still being discovered and mostly now published, testifies to the extremely active literary production on the part of the Essenes at their centre at Qumran, mostly in the century or so before the Christian era. Anyone who has visited the site will remember the large ground-plan of their *scriptorium,* where Bibles were copied and the extensive spiritual literature approved of by the sect was turned out (it must be said) almost on a scale of mass-production. Experts who study the texts have noted the contrast between the later Hebrew Bible-texts, where each letter is inscribed with care and exactitude, and the hurried style of the Qumran copyists.

The particular story I mean has not attracted very much attention, despite the fact that its original editor and translator pointedly made reference to its similarity to the Gospel infancy chapters, especially Matthew's. The problem was that it has no virgin birth, and that it is about Noah, who (except in the general sense that he like everyone is supposed to be descended from Noah after the Flood) has no very obvious link to Jesus. As a result, few people looked at it very closely. Yet it hides evidence for the real background of the Gospel story that we must work patiently and step by step to uncover — as we shall see.

But how might such a story be relevant?

Let us return to the budding author in the family, and the idea of someone doing research into the side-branches of the genealogical tree, uncovering a number of cases of literary talent not immediately obvious from the closer relatives and forebears. And now let us extend the example by supposing that the young prodigy grows up to become famous — but not for writing. He becomes, after all and to the disappointment of the bookish second aunt who encouraged him, a famous rugby-player. One can imagine the family discussions, happy as all are that the youth has achieved his glory, focussing on the surprise change of direction: and various stories being told concerning episodes which did, in retrospect, show his future sporting prowess, as when he kicked the ball on sports-day clean over the school-house. A very trivial incident such as this might come to be a 'telling' indication — or at least, be worked hard to prove that those in the know should see it as such. An incident that would have been passed over (many boys have kicked balls over the roof) had he become an author, is picked out in retrospect.

Now ancient biographers work in a way that is much closer to anecdotal and family history than our modern ones. It is tempting to say they were cruder in their approach, compared to the psychological insight and painstaking research of our researchers today; but the reality is more nearly that the modern notion of finding out everything about an individual and heaping it together would simply have made little sense in antiquity. The ancient world was simply not so interested in individuals as is our own extraordinarily individualistic culture. They would not have found it significant to know all the things we today obsessively want to know. As we have seen, a person was shaped and defined, at least in all that was acknowledged and accepted as his identity, much more by the society he belonged to. A biography of a person naturally reflected the sort of things people felt were significant, and these tended to be defined by the end of the story rather than the beginning. Already the classical Greek poet Pindar celebrates great sporting victories in the Olympic and other games, and looks back to the heroic ancestry that the victor's family claims, seeing it confirmed in the present moment of triumph. Somewhat more individualistically, the greatest of the Greek biographers, Plutarch, tells us that in his *Lives* of Greek and Roman statesmen or generals he looked out for some typical anecdote or episode that indicated the quality of an Alexander the Great, etc. We are thus made to feel that we recognize, in a telling incident, what made him the man who conquered the known world. It is chosen deliberately in the light of the achievement which was to make the man celebrated. It would have made no sense to Plutarch to have shown that the personality of Alexander contained other matter irrelevant, or contrary to his subsequent role.

The tendency is the very opposite of our private scrutinies of public figures, which sometimes crosses the boundary of legitimate curiosity. But just like our leaning in the personal and private direction, the ancient tendency could be carried to considerable lengths, and even in the end to what one can only term a degree of pathology. A man's life was supposed to reveal the basis of the achievement for which he became known. In the case of a philosopher, the life might be called upon to explain the ideas or literally to embody them even in a fantastic stretching of plausibility — as when the 'weeping philosopher,' Heraclitus, who said that 'everything is in flux (lit. flows),' was said to have died of a terrible rheum and running cold. A warped sense of poetic justice? Perhaps. But it is only an extreme case of the principle that the things which are important about a life are those which explain its known significance (producing a conqueror, a thinker). We noted how family anecdotes might work certain incidents hard, fitting them into a pattern that could really only be imposed long afterwards. Ancient biography similarly shades over into selective synthesizing of events, picking out, highlighting incidents, to fit a stylized pattern of 'the hero,' the 'pessimistic philosopher,' etc.

Plutarch's (to us) rather odd idea of *Parallel Lives,* to give his work its proper title, goes back to this idea that a great man approximates to one out of a range of such exemplary types. The two figures he has chosen each time are versions, in a way, of the same underlying figure — even the same life: the incidents in it show that he is a version of The Statesman, The Orator, or whatever. (Of course I simplify: the range of types belonging to

Graeco-Roman culture was rich and sensitive, and to comprehend it we must learn to discern its subtleties. It did not cut down
historical figures to arbitrary size, but was a way of expressing
often deep insights into what made them the great ones that they
were.)

It is still easy to say that this is to distort the person who 'actually' lived. Yet it is doubtful whether the historical person who
lived the life could himself have thought of it in any other way.
We moderns like to think that all our psychological tendencies,
all our experiences, all our potential talents, are part of us. We
must accept in return that life becomes, as a novelist said, 'a
parcel of nonsensical contingencies.' We find ourselves to be the
product of random happenings and a mixture of factors coming
over from the past. But to the ancient mentality, one's life was
the fulfilling of a destiny. It needed to be recognized, divined (*we*
might call this working the indications hard!), but some particular
incident could be a 'sign,' and lead us to see the pattern we were
supposed to fulfil. Or a biographer could present a life in the light
of that destiny.

Nowadays we know that the Gospels are touched by some
of the influences that affected Greek biography. But the Jewish
world was moving sometimes in the same direction, with its
own characteristic emphases to add. The Jews developed such
forms as those *Testaments of the Patriarchs* which we mentioned
among the Essenes. In these *Testaments,* the old patriarchs such
as Jacob and his sons, who founded the twelve tribes of Israel,
are shown looking back over the events of their lives (retold
from the Bible) — and looking into the future, prophetically, as
on their deathbed they address their children. Such works were
being written about the time of Christian origins in Syria and
thereabouts. Here too life is looked at and found meaningful not
'as it unfolds,' but precisely in retrospect and prophetically (the
present = the moment of approaching death, and so is a nothing).
Looking back, each patriarch finds that his life has brought out
a specific virtue; and looking forward, each is able to illuminate
the future as it will be in accordance with God's will which he is

able already to divine. Christians also used the form: remember Stephen's martyrdom-speech in the Acts of the Apostles. Before dying, he looks back on the past meaning of sacred history of which he feels he comes at the culminating part, and also forward to the fulfilment, the coming of the Son of Man in the clouds of heaven.

All this is needed to prepare us for Jesus, and for a tale about Noah's birth. For it helps indicate to us, though far removed from our usual modern perspectives, that looking back on someone's life meant to the ancients a sort of divining of his destiny. It was a sort of searching for the pattern which he was expected to fulfil. And in that way it was also a sort of prophetic indication.

If we are really interested in knowing how the evangelists expected their work to be read, therefore, we should be aware of the approach likely to be taken by their readers. We have already seen that the stories of Jesus' parents and the angelic visitation would have suggested the kind of Jewish literature of the visionary sects, like the Essenes and Therapeutae. If they followed the expectations thus aroused, it would be natural to find in the stories told about Jesus' childhood a bringing-out of some religious-biographical type, or particular story-pattern, which would serve to indicate what his life, so to speak, would also later express and bring to fulfilment. It might be that we would find, in what is told about him, clear parallels to other figures, such as Moses, or Noah — they both, so to speak, in some way exemplify the same type of biography. The stories about Jesus' childhood will certainly be stories about his destiny to become the saviour and redeemer of humankind — not about anything that 'just happened.' As I have indicated, the handling of these typical biographies was a sort of exact science, with its subtleties and its own complex range of meanings, in the ancient world both Jewish and Greek. In a world less accustomed to concepts and ideas, telling stories about people or things was a richly developed art that communicated much that was essential about them.

Our knowledge is often hampered by the paucity of material. The Gospels have suffered in this way particularly, as so little of the religious literature of their time has survived — or had done, until the Dead Sea Scrolls were uncovered. With the enormous mass of new material which they provide, however, we finally have some insight into (among other things) the type of story which was told in these mystic circles about the great ones of sacred history: stories which were a way, in a time before the highly conceptualized thinking of today, of catching the essential quality of a hero or a saint. It is in this context that we may approach the fascinating parallels which emerge between the so-called *Genesis Apocryphon* from Cave 1 at Qumran, written in Aramaic in the first or second century BC, and the Gospel of Matthew. Like the already mentioned *Book of Jubilees,* it is a special retelling of parts of the Bible, and the section which concerns us is the earliest surviving fragment, concerned with the birth of Noah (column 2 in the original Hebrew text). It is a story with a sensational, not to say scandalous implication, and contains some surprisingly uninhibited dialogue.

Noah's parents in the document are Lamech and Bathenosh, and it is Lamech who tells the story. The pregnancy has evidently just been reported to him when the fragment begins — or it may be that the child has just been born. At any rate Lamech is highly disturbed:

> My heart was troubled within me because of this child.
> Then I, Lamech, approached Bathenosh [my] wife in haste
> and said to her: 'By the Most High, by the great Lord, by
> the King of all worlds, until you tell me all things truthfully,
> if .... Tell me this [truthfully] and do not lie, ... By the King
> of all worlds, until you tell me truthfully and not falsely ...'

His repetitive speech vividly captures his irrational, jealous state of mind. But his wife is angry at the insinuation that the child might not be his, and reminds him of a particular passionate moment:

Then Bathenosh my wife spoke to me in great indignation, [and] said, 'My brother, my lord, remember my pleasure ... (remember) our lying together, and my soul within its body (?). And [I tell you] all things truthfully.

My heart was still greatly troubled within me, and when Bathenosh my wife saw that my countenance had changed .... She mastered her anger and spoke to me, saying 'My lord, my brother, remember my pleasure! I swear to you by the Holy One, the King of [the heavens], ... that this seed is yours, and that this conception is from you. This fruit was planted by you, and by no stranger or Watcher or Son of Heaven. ... Why is your countenance changed and dismayed, and why is your spirit thus distressed?... I speak to you truthfully.'

We notice that the style already tends somewhat in the direction of *Joseph and Asenath.* The writer's interest lies in the portrayal of human situations, involving romantic passions of love and jealousy, though the religious setting is just as prominent. Despite Bathenosh's appeal to their love-life and softened tone, Lamech is still unsure that the child is his. But before doing anything, he wants to hear from Enoch — the great authority among these esoteric sects, and a figure who is often tinged with the supernatural, having powers of prophecy and knowledge of divine secrets. Here he is mentioned as a sort of oracular being, rather than a mere human ancestor (though he is Lamech's grandfather). Lamech sends his own father, Methuselah, to find out the truth from Enoch, which turns out to mean travelling to the mysterious land of Parwain at the ends of the earth.

The characterization of Enoch is important. It is said that 'he shared the lot [of the angels], who taught him all things.' This is a phrase that we meet elsewhere in the Dead Sea Scrolls. The Essenes were governed by Council of the higher religious dignitaries, who had already progressed through the elementary stages of the holy life. It is of them that we hear:

Thou wilt bring the glory of thy salvation
    to all the men of thy Council,
    to those who share the lot
    of the Angels of the Countenance.

(from Hymn 10 in the *Thanksgiving Scroll*)

Those in the higher echelons of the Essene Order, then, already lived the pure life of the angels and of the world-to-come, and likewise shared their higher knowledge. For they stand before the Countenance of God. Enoch is being presented as one who has left the world to live the life of an 'angel,' or one might equally say of an archetypal Essene initiate.

From him, Methuselah learns the reassuring truth that Lamech's son is not sinfully begotten, but is his father's true offspring. We know this because, where the fragment of the *Apocryphon* breaks off, its content fortunately dovetails into a story we know from the *Book of Enoch* (*1 Enoch* 106). In this continuation, Enoch says that he has seen the truth in a vision, and sends a message back via Methuselah to Lamech:

Make known to your son Lamech that the son who has
been born is indeed righteous, and call his name Noah ...
and he and his sons shall be saved from the corruption that
shall come upon the earth.

The Enochic story also casts light on the reasons for Lamech's perplexity.

The shorter version in *Enoch* lacks the scene between Lamech and Bathenosh, however, so that it will be best to pause here and consider the implications of what we know so far. It is undoubtedly reminiscent of Matthew's Joseph and Mary, in just the same way that *Joseph and Asenath* reminded us of a Gospel scene. There is an unexpected child, a father who thinks that the child cannot be his, a (potential) breakdown of the relationship, then a reassuring message from an angel, a vision/dream in which the truth is revealed, and with it a charge to give the child a certain name and an indication of his special destiny. Once again, this story is certainly not in any simplistic sense the source of the Gospel, because it lacks other features such as the virgin birth itself. But we are slowly starting to build up a competence in reading the sort of visionary language of symbol and story that would have been familiar to readers when the Gospels were written, and guided their understanding of what was really meant.

A little angel

The story in the Dead Sea Scrolls is the closest actual parallel to the Gospel of Matthew's infancy chapter that is so far known, and comes from a setting close to it in space and time. What can we infer, then, about its intended message?

We need first of all to comprehend more clearly the grounds of Lamech's anxiety, which emerge much more directly in the Enochic version of the story, even though the more summary style lacks the dramatic dialogue of Bathenosh and her husband. In both versions, Bathenosh is subject to the accusation that she has had relations either with a (human) 'stranger,' or with a 'Son of Heaven,' also termed a 'Watcher.' In *1 Enoch*'s version it is revealed why Lamech has become suspicious. For we learn about the birth of the child, and the newborn's certainly most remarkable appearance:

> His body was white as snow and red as a rose, and he had hair on his head that was white like snow, and his thick curls were beautiful. And when he opened his eyes, the whole house shone like the sun — or even more exceedingly ...
>
> And his father, Lamech, was afraid of him and fled and went to his father Methuselah, and said to him, 'I have begotten a strange son. He is not like a human being, but he looks like the children of the angels of heaven to me ... His

eyes are like the rays of the sun, and his face is glorious. It
does not seem to me that he is from me, but from the angels, and I fear that some awful thing may take place upon
the earth in his days. So I am beseeching you now, begging
you in order that you may go to Enoch, our father, and
learn from him the truth, for his dwelling-place is among
the angels.'

And so off Methuselah goes to visit Enoch, who is himself a
quasi-angelic being just as in the Dead Sea Scrolls text.

Lamech is worried, then, that his child is a portent, a supernatural phenomenon, and not his own son. Again, oddly close to
the Gospel story — where Jesus indeed is a supernatural child!
He thinks he may be some kind of offspring of the angels. This
in turn is still closer to an apocryphal version of the infancy-story,
which is to be found in a beautiful but curious text called the
Protevangelium.

The 'Gospel of the First Part of Jesus' Life,' as we might
render the Greek term, was written sometime soon after AD 150,
and was extremely popular in the Middle Ages. It is really much
more about the Virgin Mary than it is about Jesus, but it covers
the actual birth stories of the Gospels, and treats them in what
the scholars have always thought was a very imaginative and free
manner. Some differences in emphasis are particularly striking.
Where Matthew glossed over the human drama of jealousy and
anger, to go straight for his theological point, the *Protevangelium*
tells a fuller and more emotive tale. Joseph returns from work one
day and realizes that his 'virgin' wife is pregnant:

He entered his house and found her with child. And he
smote his face, threw himself down on sackcloth, and
wept bitterly, saying: 'With what countenance shall I look
towards the Lord my God? What prayer shall I offer for this
'maiden'? For I received her out of the Temple of the Lord
my God, and have not protected her. Who has deceived me?
Who has done this evil in my house and defiled her?'

Theology is not far off, for Joseph likens himself to Adam fatefully leaving Eve alone, when the serpent seduced her. But it is his humiliating betrayal and her crime which are the focus of his hurt and anger. And the situation is developed with an apparently novelistic interest rather than a theological eye as he confronts her and demands answers:

> And Joseph arose from the sackcloth and called Mary and said to her, 'You who are cared for by God, why have you done this and forgotten the Lord your God? Why have you debased your soul, you who were brought up in the Holy of Holies and received food from the hand of an angel?'
>
> But she wept bitterly and said, 'I am pure and I know not a man.'
>
> And Joseph said to her, 'Whence then is this in your womb?'
>
> And she said, 'As the Lord my God lives, I do not know whence it has come to me.'
>
> And Joseph feared greatly, and went away from her, pondering what he should do with her.

Fortunately, in the night following, an angel comes to Joseph in a dream and tells him (in the words of Matthew's Gospel): 'Do not fear because this child,' and reveals to him that it will be a saviour of the people from their sins.

It used to be thought that the *Protevangelium* was no more than a later elaboration of the canonical Gospels — and much of it probably is just that. But after studying the *Genesis Apocryphon*'s story of Lamech and Bathenosh, it seems possible that at least some elements of it were building on older ideas. And this is strikingly confirmed when he take note of Joseph's deepest fears over the child:

> And Joseph said, 'If I conceal her sin, I shall be found opposing the Law of the Lord. If I expose her to the children of Israel, I fear lest that which is in her may have sprung from the angels ...'

That is not a theory which could have come out of normal Christian theology! It is at any rate possible that its author was using older versions of the Jesus story, which also underlay but are toned down in the Gospel of Matthew: at least, his source seems to be a version of the same story, but including elements such as the scenes of jealousy and protestation between Joseph and Mary, the idea that the child might be an angel-offspring, which belong to the older tale, witnessed in the Dead Sea Scrolls' account of Noah. But could Matthew really have been using a story that was originally narrated of Noah?

Actually, it is quite in accord with Matthew's theology to see a parallel between the destiny of Jesus and the time of Noah, when the Flood suddenly swept away an unsuspecting and sinful generation. Jesus himself prophesies later in Matthew (24:37–9):

> As were the days of Noah, so shall be the coming of the
> Son of Man. For as in those days which were before the
> Flood, they were eating and drinking, marrying and giving
> in marriage ... so shall be the coming of the Son of Man.

This prophetic usage of the catastrophic Flood to suggest the similarly impending Judgment in the time of Jesus agrees closely with Lamech's foreboding that his extraordinary child portends some dreadful event to happen 'in his days.' To portray Jesus' birth as like that of Noah would exemplify perfectly that way we noticed in ancient 'biography' that a story is made to indicate the coming destiny of the child. Enoch prophesied that Noah and his sons would 'be saved from the corruption of those days,' indeed he will be the saviour of the human race which would otherwise be wiped out. So Jesus is destined to bring the divine Judgment, and his birth marks him as one like Noah who stands on the brink of a great turning-point in history.

The world of such ideas is not that of later Christian theology, but it is just the sort of conception that we find in the Dead Sea Scrolls and among the esoteric sects. The birth of a prophetic figure, such as Jesus is portrayed, would be the sign of a new age. Such a birth is itself a divine 'message,' as an angel is a divine 'messenger.' Such a birth is God telling us, if we will understand (as do the initiated, like Enoch, like the Essenes, but unlike the worldly with their marrying and giving in marriage, their eating and drinking), of a coming time of crisis and decision.

There is also something disturbing, however, in the 'angelic' theory of the wonder-child's birth. For on the whole it is not good angels who are said in the Bible to be involved in the begetting of human children, but bad ones.

The Watchers

In the Old Testament, we recall, it was the Watcher angels — or fallen angels — who saw the daughters of men, 'that they were fair,' and produced children on them. Such children were 'Giants,' heroes, but hardly the central figures of the biblical history. Or to put it another way, the important spiritual leaders in the Old Testament are not miraculously-born heroes or supernatural prodigies, but particular men, in themselves like other men but chosen and guided by God, like Abraham, or Moses, or the prophets: the stories of heroes and 'divine' miracle-children belonged more to the pagan Mysteries. Even late into historical times, the Greeks continued to believe in heroes. Such men were regarded in paganism as divinely sent to inspire new civilizations, found nations or to begin new cycles of time. Seen from the Jewish perspective, however, they were not so much as godlike, as Luciferic — seizing the prerogatives of divinity while being less than truly divine. In the Bible it is God who chooses his special people, and who governs the ebb and flow of nations. Figures like Alexander the Great or his Successors seemed to Judaism not men raised to godhead, but paraders of usurped divine power. To claim divine-angelic origin and inspiration in this way was to show that the powers involved were opposed to the true God, stealing his glory.

The case was not quite so simple, however. We recall that the Essenes had a theory of the 'double revelation.' Its profounder thought was that all wisdom comes ultimately from God. The Jewish religion certainly told of the true God; but if there was validity in the insights of pagan philosophy and science, or in the values of pagan civilization, it could only be because they were stolen from the true source. Luciferic wisdom was indeed stolen from the mysteries of heaven, by the 'fallen angels.' But in its original, pure form it is and must also be found in a deeper, esoteric understanding of the Old Testament revelation. And that full, original wisdom is the key to the future reunification of humankind, when Judaism will bring become the Law of all humanity. The Essenes and like-minded groups were remarkably open to pagan influences, both from the Greek world and from oriental ideas, notably from Iran and its religion of Light and Darkness.

In effect they were making a new synthesis of knowledge — but they were convinced they were only restoring what was known originally to the patriarchs and primordial figures of the Bible. They elaborated esoteric 'Mysteries,' like those of Egypt or Greece, which led people to spiritual awakening through ritual and meditation; we know much about them now from the Dead Sea Scrolls. But they believed that the pagan Mysteries were here being restored to their true role, that of serving the God of the Bible rather than the Luciferic powers, the false gods, who in mythological terms had stolen heavenly secrets and tried to turn them to their own selfish ends. Whatever the mythology, the meaning of the new historical fusion was clear. Such esoteric groups claimed that they were able to resist the 'temptation' of falling back into paganism, and were able to give the pagan spirituality a new, forward-looking direction in terms of their own vision of a dawning 'new age.' They themselves were aware, however, that they were dealing with forces that could easily be misinterpreted, or that could lead astray those who failed to comprehend the whole vision of the future in which they took their place.

Lamech was rightly worried, then, about Bathenosh his wife, and the possibility that she had been communing with false, Luciferic angels. Once again there is considerable similarity to the situation of *Joseph and Aseneth.* There the pagan princess enacted a Mystery that led from paganism to the true religion, that of Joseph her destined Lord, the 'man of God.' Bathenosh is not a gentile, but she is giving birth to a wonder-child, who will rescue humanity, and who seems to be born more in the manner of a pagan hero than a biblical patriarch. The jealousy and anxiety of Lamech is an expression therefore of a much larger concern among the Jewish esoteric sects: their anxiety of losing the touchstone of the biblical faith, their adherence to the true God. Being open to pagan ideas, yet trusting that they will reveal the deeper meaning implicit in the Bible, they run the risk of lapsing into the pagan version of their own teaching — or, at the least, of appearing to lead the people after false gods. When Enoch gives his reassuring prophecy for Methuselah to take back to Lamech, we can now understand why he speaks precisely about the way that humankind before the Flood had been led astray by the Watcher angels and their stolen wisdom. They have all sinned. But Noah, he says, will be found righteous in his generation (a biblical phrase). In other words, when the pagan, fallen wisdom is swept away, Noah will carry forward the spiritual wisdom in its future form — that is what is meant, it seems, by saving his people from their sins, that is, from following false wisdom rather than the true.

In the Bible's original concept of the Messiah there was nothing about a virgin-born miracle-worker. The child born to Mary in Matthew's Gospel is thus stretching the bounds of what could be comprehended from traditional Jewish ideas even more. We have already suggested that Matthew meant to challenge ideas and bring his readers to so great a 'discovery,' the significance of Jesus, that it required the Bible, the truth of former times, itself to be reinterpreted. That is exactly what gives the meaning to a 'miracle,' that it changes our thinking rather than fitting old categories. Mary is not a gentile — though she is from Galilee, symbolically opposed to the traditional centre, Jerusalem and the Temple, in the Gospel tradition. But the condensed version of the 'Noah' story told about Joseph and Mary indicates, in the terms of spiritual story and esoteric romance, that her child requires us to cross the bounds of existing beliefs. Even those most intimately involved in the new step forward in humankind's spiritual evolution, it suggests, cannot avoid the inner crises and tensions, uncertainties and fear of losing their established identities. They must inevitably worry that in the new fusion of ideas, the essential truth of the Bible may be lost in a pagan takeover.

In no version of the tale, however, does it turn out that the woman really has been involved with Luciferic tendencies/ angels. The one who is born is instead the guarantee that humanity will be led to the true, saving knowledge. In Matthew there is the angel's speech of reassurance, which presumably is adapted too from the older versions where it is spoken by Enoch, himself an 'angelic' being. Interestingly, its wording is not quite the same as Matthew's own earlier intervention ('by the Holy Spirit,' i.e. in accordance with God's purposes). The angel says, very literally, in the Greek, 'The child begotten in her is through a spirit which is holy,' and it may well be wrong to see here a theological reference to Jesus' divinity, or the Holy Spirit. The phrase still contains an echo from the source-legend of the reassurance that the one-to-be-born was not a throwback to a sinful past, but a hope for a new age to come. And we may agree that Jesus, at the very least, fitted that bill.

3. Jesus as Noah

A golden boy

Following the trail of Joseph and Mary's quarrel has brought us to a story about a wonder-child, disruptive and disturbing as much as amazing in his appearance. In the *Genesis Apocryphon* and *1 Enoch* he is Noah, destined to be a light to his generation who have abandoned the way of wisdom and fallen into sin. To the imagination of the visionary who reinterpreted the Bible, in these and similar works of Essenes or their predecessors, he already shone with significance in his childhood when he first opened his eyes. In his very birth, his destiny was revealed. Jesus in the tradition of Matthew's Gospel is a child of this kind, and a version of the same tale is told of him there and in its apocryphal variations. But to understand him, the Bible had to be read with deeper insight, of the special kind that the Essenes above all specialized in providing. So new and challenging were their readings of the Bible's deeper sense that they provoked anxiety and the danger of a break with Jewish tradition — reflected in the fear Lamech has about his wife, that she may have been communing with sinful, paganizing spirits. For a miraculous birth was what normally took place in myths from the pagan Mysteries, reflected in their myths about the 'divine child.' But could these conceptions be brought into the more historical, literal and legal religion of Judaism without blowing it apart? And where did the Essenes derive their 'Mystery' ideas, that seemed to them so important as a link to the wider future of humankind?

Fortunately, the answer to the last question is one that has become much clearer since the Dead Sea Scrolls were found. Such ideas came especially from ancient Iran.

The Dead Sea Scrolls are revealing in many ways. They have brought us biblical texts that are centuries older than any previously known, for example. But they are astounding in another way, for their non-biblical affinities. No-one expected that a prominent Jewish-mystical movement like the Essenes would turn out so different from 'biblical' expectations. Yet it soon became clear that in contrast to the historical and national religion of the Old Testament, the Essenes had a cosmic religion, based on their conception of man's (potential) role in the universe, as God's steward, so to speak, on earth, and the expectation of a future transformation when the earth would be renewed and made as God had intended it to be, before sin 'marred all.' Passages in the Dead Sea Scrolls portrayed humanity as a part of a greater order — that of the divine Light. But the world had been partly taken over by the powers of Darkness. Humanity was required to play its part in the struggle against them. We remember that the Essenes saw themselves as standing alongside and in the company of the angels: so they themselves were a sort of extra hierarchy of the divine hosts, working with the powers who governed the cosmos.

Ideas like these cannot have come from the Bible. Rather it was soon noticed that in many details they echoed the religious teachings of Zoroastrianism, the 'Religion of Light' which had originally been taught in Iran many millennia previously by Zoroaster or Zarathustra — and survives to this day in India, and in pockets elsewhere. Nowadays it is a small religion in numbers: but at the beginning of the Christian era it was the religion of the powerful Parthian Empire, the successor to the celebrated Empire of the Persians and Medes. Over centuries of imperial conquests, it had been spread widely throughout the Middle East. The archaic prophet of Iran had taught of the 'Wise Lord,' Ahura Mazdah, whose name was later contracted to the form Ohrmazd. He was the God of Light, of ultimate Truth, and of right-order (*asha*). Everything creative and living and good and true in the universe was an expression of his being, and man too was one of his creatures. But he was opposed by another, co-eternal being of Darkness, the 'agonized' or negative spirit, Angra Mainyush, later shortened to Ahriman. Everything to do with death and decay and corruption was an expression of the fact that he had 'invaded' the bright, living world and hardened it, dragging it down toward death and inertia. Humanity was on the front line between the two spirits, and it was our task to co-operate with the Light. Agriculture, for example, was not a merely a material business, to be done in order to feed ourselves better; it was part of a transforming work designed to bring more light and life into the world, overcoming the tendency of the material domain toward hardening and death. By good thoughts, good deeds and good words humanity performed a priestlike task of bringing forward the evolution of the earth.

If 'evolution' sounds too modern an idea, the world-process is nevertheless exactly so described in some of the most ancient texts, which tell how the living-and-growing reality of the Light, and the world it created, will one day develop so far that it will overcome the tendency to death and inertia (Ahriman) altogether. The Darkness or materializing principle will then cease to be, and the world will be all Light, — it will be 'Transfigured' as the Zoroastrians say. 'May we be among those who bring about the Transfiguration of the earth!' is still a fervent prayer of Zarathustra's religionists today.

The notion that the Darkness will be overcome, and that there can be evolution, might seem to contradict the statement that the Dark is an eternal reality alongside the Light. Zoroastrianism put forward, however, a brilliant metaphysical account of the struggle of the two Spirits, according to which Ahriman is, in his essence, retardation. Now, whenever there is forward movement there is the simultaneous possibility of its being held back or impeded; the two conceptions — the creative thrust of the Light, the impeding power of Ahriman — therefore belong logically, eternally, together. On the other hand, if the Light struggles against the impeding force of the Dark power and finally attains its full unfolding, at that point all retardation has been overcome and therefore Ahriman no longer exists. In more pictorial and mythical language, it was said that Ohrmazd challenged Ahriman to a contest *in time*. Ahriman foolishly, unforeseeingly (since he is backwardness itself) agreed; when he was defeated in time, his eternal potential to retard no longer existed — and nor did he. That time is not yet, though, but has only been revealed in a prophetic vision by Ohrmazd to his prophet.

Humanity needs to have such a revelation if it is to play its part in the struggle. Indeed, it can play its part only if the Light ever and again receives the commitment of human beings to fight for Light and order against death and degeneration. Whenever they fail in their spiritual duty, they are giving in to the waiting forces of Darkness, ever ready to invade. Ohrmazd has sent a succession of heroes and prophets to reinforce the message of the Light to human beings: so that we are at once able to see some of the most important concepts of Zoroastrianism in their mutual connection. Firstly, there is the vision of a cosmic process with a direction in time, guided toward the Transfiguration but requiring man's help to bring it to realization. Every human being must therefore make a *decision* to help in the struggle. That decision must be renewed throughout history by the whole succession of human beings, so the revelation is also renewed and reinforced by a succession of prophets and heroes.

By fighting Ahriman in time, Ohrmazd at first seems to be giving the world over (at least in part) to the forces of Darkness — indeed the struggle against evil becomes more and more intense — but only temporarily, in order finally to overcome them once and for all. At the last stage, just before the Transfiguration, Ohrmazd will send a great teacher and fighter-for-the-Light, who will be in effect a 'World-Saviour,' called the Saoshyant. Every other teacher and hero is in a sense no more than an anticipation of that final Saviour — not excluding Zarathustra himself. In fact, because the Saoshyant is the fulfiller of Zarathustra's vision and completes his mission, he is seen as a kind of reappearance, or even the completion, of Zarathustra. The same truth that was known prophetically to Zarathustra in the form of a future victory will be a present reality in the Saoshyant. Included in the very content of the message is the fact that it needs to be revealed, and receive man's commitment, ever anew. This intimate link between Zarathustra, the revealer, and the message he reveals, will be important later to understanding his importance, as it suggests that Zarathustra somehow accompanies humankind through history. So too will be the fact that the Saoshyant, or World-Saviour, is prophesied to be born of a virgin!

Far-reaching indeed were the cosmic and prophetological ideas that had grown up in Zoroastrianism. The Essenes of the Dead Sea Scrolls borrowed from Zoroastrianism the notion of history as a struggle between Light and Dark, the demand for commitment and a human role in cosmic evolution. They borrowed also the idea of a Future World where death and darkness had been overcome, as the greater goal of religious evolution. Thus much is accepted nowadays by all scholars of the Dead Sea Scrolls and contemporary Jewish thought. Would it be surprising if they were influenced also by the concept of the Saoshyant — the coming World-Saviour who heralds the triumph of the Light? And could he through their channels of influence have affected Christian thought about a virgin-born Messiah?

We can prove that indeed they were influenced — but not quite in the straightforward way that one might like history to work. History does seem to have a habit of being somewhat less than straightforward, even devious. Nevertheless it turns out perhaps to be much more interesting that way. What we can prove is that the Essenes who retold the story we have examined in *1 Enoch* and in the *Genesis Apocryphon* were in touch with stories from the Zoroastrian world about one of their heroes. He is not, however, the final Hero, but a lesser one — the hero Zal, also known as 'golden Zal.'

The legends and myths of archaic Iran were not written down until a late date, because they were originally oral tradition and heroic saga. The Persian epic poet Firdausi wrote them down in the ninth century AD in his *Shahnameh* or 'Epic of the Kings' — probably because the oral tradition was fading, as Iran became Islamicized. He tells the story of the birth of Zal, son to a famous father, the hero Kereshasp the Saman, a notable dragon-slayer. As it unfolds, the story suggests analogies that belong to the typical world of ideas we have sketched from the Zoroastrian background. The legend is not just about the past, but also anticipates the future, for Kereshasp is destined to be resurrected at the time of the Transfiguration and will kill the mythical Ahrimanic embodiment, half-man half-dragon, called Azidahak (in Firdausi, Zahhak). Kereshasp thus resembles the Saoshyant in some ways. In the Zoroastrian version he is to be the great helper of the World-Saviour — or perhaps we will come to think that the doctrine of the Saoshyant is really a kind of symbolic-prophetic resumé of the entire process by which the heroes of Light have fought against the Darkness and will eventually defeat it, throughout history. In Zoroastrianism, all the old mythology is seen as being fulfilled in the Future World, and so is given a specifically Zoroastrian meaning. In mythic terms, therefore, it is appropriately to Kereshasp that the coming of the Saoshyant is promised by the prophet, Zarathustra himself.

Meantime, back to the story: Kereshasp has a son, who is to fight against the dragon-king Azidahak even though he cannot yet kill him. However, in a turn of events which may sound similar to a story we have studied already, Kereshasp the Saman (called Sam in Firdausi), has grave doubts about the strange appearance and uncertain origins of the child when he is born. He initially rejects him, and has to travel to receive an oracle from a magic bird (cf. angel, etc.) called the Simurgh, which lives in the remote mountains of the Elburz. Sound familar?

In many telling details, in fact, right down to the specific feature of the child's shocking white hair at birth, we may recognize in the legend of Zal the story that was applied in *1 Enoch* and the Dead Sea Scrolls to the figure of Noah. And if additional evidence were needed, we know that the story was in circulation because, without so much detail but in unmistakable outline, it also turns up in a work called the *Apocalypse of Adam* — considered by some scholars as pre-Christian, or written just about the time of Christian beginnings. It too places the story in a series of events immediately following after the Flood. We will have more to say about the *Apocalypse of* Adam later. But here first are the main tellings of the story set out in parallel:

1 Enoch 106–7	Zal (*Shahnameh* trans. R. Levy pp.35–39)
Lamech's wife bears him a son of strange appearance: (106:1)	Sām (Kereshasp) fathers a son of strange appearance:
'And his hair was white like wool ... and when he opened his eyes all the house glowed like the sun, or even more exceedingly.' (106:2).	'When the child was severed from his mother his face was beautiful like the sun but his hair was entirely white.'
Lamech 'was afraid of him and fled and ... said: I have begotten a strange son; he is not like a human being, but like the children of the [evil] angels.' (106:4–5)	'On seeing his son thus, with his white hair, Sām in great fear ... strayed' and said: 'My blackened soul writhes with shame because of this child which ... resembles a child of Ahriman.'
(*Genesis Ap.*): 'I thought within my heart that conception was (due) to the Watchers and ... to the *nephilim;*' then follows the dialogue in which Lamech rebukes his wife, and she protests her innocence.	
He rejects the child, (106:6)	He casts out the child which is brought up by the Simurgh in the Elburz mountains.
and sends Methuselah to visit Enoch on the mountain of Paradise	Subsequently Sām comes to the mountain. He prays:

at the ends of the earth, 'for his
dwelling place is among the
angels.' (106:7)

There he 'cried aloud and I
[Enoch] came to him.' (106:8)

He tells him that Lamech 'did not   'If this child indeed comes from
believe the child was his, but of the   my loins undefiled and not from the
image of the angels'(106:12)   seed of evil souled Ahriman, then
                                           help thy servant ascend here ...'

Enoch assures him that   Simurgh restores the child, and
                                           promises that if called on, 'I will
                                           come, like a storm cloud, with
                                           speed.'

                                           The Simurgh (in *Apocalypse of
                                           Adam:* an angel which 'came
he has seen in a vision (106:13)   forth,' i.e. in a vision) promises that
                                           he will be a great world-ruler.

that 'the son who has been born is
indeed righteous ... and (you shall)   Sām bestows on the child the name
call his name Noah' (106:18)   Zal, or 'golden Zal.'

'and he shall be saved from ... all   He will fight against the world-
the sin and oppression ... and it will   domination of the evil Azidahak.
be fulfilled upon the earth in his
days. And after that shall occur still
greater oppression ...' (106:18f)

'And each generation shall be more   Azidahak cannot be finally
wicked than the other, until a right-   defeated until the end-time, when
eous generation shall arise. Then,   Sām will rise again when he will
sin shall disappear from on earth ....'   destroy him at the 'Transfiguration'
(107:1)   of the earth.

Several features of the tale in *Enoch* and the Dead Sea Scrolls become easier to understand when we know the original on which the legend was based. The young hero under the protection of the fabulous bird, the Simurgh, became Noah who is watched over by the mysterious, oracular figure of Enoch. There were rather more ancestors in between than the story really required, hence the duplication of roles with Lamech sending Methuselah rather than going to ask Enoch himself, as one would expect of an anxious father. Enoch himself was transposed to a 'mountain,' which is not usually where he is to be found, because the high Elburz mountain-range was in the Zoroastrian mythology a place of mystery and revelation, inhabited by magic beings like the Simurgh. In the *Apocalypse of Adam* version, the Simurgh has also been interpreted as an 'angel' which appears in a vision.

The story also makes sense in a more profound way, because we can appreciate how the *Book of Enoch* and the Essenes were using it: to bring out a deeper meaning, as they saw it, from the biblical narrative about Noah.

The Bible basically tells how God punished sinful humanity with destruction, but spared Noah who was 'righteous in his generation' (Gen.6:9) and made a covenant with him to ensure better behaviour henceforth. The ordinary Jewish tradition was not sure that being 'righteous in his generation' was much to get excited about, and some Rabbis thought it might merely mean that considering when he lived he was not quite as bad as the rest of humanity. But the esotericists saw in the whole thing a mystery, concerned with that eternal struggle of Light and Dark. Noah became in their eyes a representative of that 'eternal knowledge' of which the Dead Sea Scrolls constantly speak, and sinful humanity at the time of the Flood stood for the false or corrupted knowledge of the 'fallen angels,' as Enoch explained to Methuselah. In the Zal-story, the hero and his father Kereshasp live in the time of the struggle against the Dark power which is ruling the earth through Azidahak, the dragon-king. The hero's only partial success in defeating the dragon-king serves to throw the real interest forward (in typical Zoroastrian fashion) to the future outcome of the struggle, when the Dark will finally be defeated in the end-time, at the Transfiguration of the earth. Likewise, the Essene version of the Noah-story is no longer about a new religious start that was made in times long gone by, but becomes an indication of the on-going metaphysical drama behind the biblical history: it too points forward to the ultimate victory of the Light and the Truth, when 'sin shall disappear from the earth.' There is certainly a step here from the Jewish religion based on their treasured national history, toward the coming Christian idea of universal redemption and renewal.

The basic notion — that the child is born as a startling revelation in a dark time — is a reflection of that absolutely fundamental idea of Zoroastrianism that, though it seems the world has been given over to darkness and struggle, this is itself part of the divine plan to ensure total victory. Those who understand realize that the strange child is one step in that process: even at his birth he vouches for the fact that the Light, exemplified in this 'golden child,' is there, even though it is hard to discern (even for his own parents!) in the hour of the prevalence of the Dark.

In Essene terms, the idea became fused with their notion that the 'sinful,' 'fallen' knowledge of the worldly powers would appear again in its true form, as already indicated mysteriously and cryptically in the Bible, when a new age dawned. Kereshasp in the prototype-story is a very ambiguous figure. According to other stories about him, he slays dragons and other evil monsters, yet in a way that often involves him in committing terrible sins. In him Darkness and Light are still mixed up. He almost commits another of his terrible sins in rejecting his child, and is able to recognize Zal as truly begotten and a fighter for the Light only after an inner struggle and a revelation from the Simurgh. Likewise in the Noah-story, the possibility of his coming from the fallen angels rather than the true lineage has to be considered before Lamech, following Enoch's vision reported to him by Methuselah, can be sure that he really belongs to the future and the good knowledge it will bring.

In such stories, the esoteric symbols come to life and generate situations of human drama and uncertainty. Behind them, however, we can discover deep spiritual convictions, for all they take the form of vision and romance. By telling a very similar story, the predecessors of the evangelist we know as Matthew can only have meant to indicate that the child Jesus was an embodiment of hope in a still dark world; that he pointed to a metaphysical victory that went beyond even what the Bible, literally speaking, had to say about the eventual outcome of history: he stood for that higher knowledge which the Essenes and similar groups treasured and believed was hidden beneath the surface-meaning of the Bible-text, which held that the Light, the spirit, is truly eternal, whereas the Darkness apparently so powerful all around us will one day be defeated and disappear for ever. Or in mythical-pictorial terms, Jesus takes his place in the long line of miraculous heroes and dragon-slayers — a notion which, we shall see, is not so absurd as it first seems.

In the stories about Zal, however, and the future victory of the World-Saviour, the miraculously born Saoshyant, the idea of the 'virgin birth' still apparently dances just out of our reach. Even now we have not been able to connect it with any story that actually affected the Gospel. However, in the *Apocalypse of Adam* the story of Zal features alongside a number of other relevant stories. One tells of a hero, or prophet of a similar type to Zal, of whom we finally hear explicitly that 'he came from a virgin womb.' We may be on the right track after all.

Jesus the dragon-slayer

The *Apocalypse of Adam* is not in the Bible. It is not in the Dead Sea Scrolls. It was not even heard of before 1945, when a group of Egyptian fellahin were digging at the foot of the mountainous cliffs edging the Nile valley. They discovered some old pots — and inside them some of the most amazing manuscripts from the early Christian centuries, now named, after the place of their discovery, the Nag Hammadi Library.

Most of the works it contains are Gnostic revelations of secret wisdom, in which Christ is mentioned as a teacher of secret doctrines and ideas that are very different from most of what we find in the Bible. But other works in the collection are interesting because they apparently preceded this 'heretical' phase, duly rejected by the Church. Much evidence now exists that the Church made the Gnostics into heretics as much by shifting its own position away from earlier Christian thought as by preserving a supposed original orthodoxy. In reality, it seems, Gnostic ideas only diverged gradually from Christianity, and both had a relationship to the sort of esoteric Judaism we have just been examining. Some of the Nag Hammadi works stand remarkably close to the mainstream of earliest Christianity, and some, like the *Apocalypse of Adam,* may have originated in the visionary Judaism of the time just beforehand, to which we have been repeatedly directing our attention. Certainly Jewish mystics, early Christians and later Gnostics all have a considerable common heritage.

It is sometimes said that the *Apocalypse of Adam* contains Gnostic ideas of the later, clearly heretical kind. But this is simply not true. For example: the Gnostics taught that this world was not made by God, but by a lesser power, even one opposed to the true Divinity. (Possibly this again reflects the Iranian-Zoroastrian notion of Ahriman, who materializes and solidifies the world. Prior to the 'mixture,' the world as it was originated by Ohrmazd would exist in a state of pure Light.) It is true that the *Apocalypse of Adam* has some hostility to the material realm, but it never calls the maker of it anything other than God — and it is clear in many passages from the document that 'God' refers to God, not a lesser power. Moreover, many Jewish-apocalyptic writings regard the lower world as hostile, or as under the (permitted) rule of evil powers, and insist that we must search for the higher, spiritual dimension that will break through and be victorious in the future. There is increasing support for the idea that the *Apocalypse of Adam* comes out of esoteric Jewish thought. The fact that it contains the story of Zal, also found in the Dead Sea Scrolls and *1 Enoch* (applied to Noah), now tends to confirm its Jewish and close-to-Essene origins. Its esoteric meaning will become clearer, indeed, as we study it against that background of ideas.

The story of Zal appears in something of catalogue of stories, twelve or thirteen in number and listed one after another with the explanation that they all refer to a mysterious figure known as 'the Illuminator.' Since they derive from twelve different 'Kingdoms' of the world, and are extended in a series starting after the Flood, they apparently indicate a series of reincarnations of the Illuminator, appearing time after time to reveal to humanity the nature of the Light. Perhaps it will be no surprise to learn that the title 'Illuminator' is one that belongs especially to the prophet of Light from ancient Iran, Zarathustra. Once again however it is not Zarathustra, or the Saoshyant, but another lesser hero whose story follows after that of Zal: the hero Faridun.

Faridun is the more recent form of an ancient name, Thraetaona. He is another dragon-slayer, like Kereshasp, Zal's father. By now, the reader may be becoming familiar with the fact that future heroes of this type tend to have a difficult childhood. Faridun is no exception. The *Apocalypse of Adam* summarizes his tale as follows:

> He came from a virgin womb. He was cast out of the city,
> he and his mother. He was taken to a desert place. He nur-
> tured himself there. He came and received glory and power.
> And thus he came on the water.

Firdausi, and several ancient sources, confirm the details. The villain of the piece is again that dragon-human king who tyrannized over ancient legendary times, Azidahak. His evil power over the world seems complete, but he has learned in a disquieting dream that his conqueror and successor is about to be born. Accordingly he sends his soldiers and agents to find him and destroy him. Meanwhile, Azidahak himself is decimating the population, because he feeds every day on children's brains! His agents of destruction however are too slow to find the child, and the family escape, except that the father is captured and killed. They leave the city and travel to foreign lands, hiding in the wilderness, where the child grows up in exile. When he comes of age, he returns to claim the kingdom from the monster-tyrant. As we know, Azidahak cannot yet be killed — but he can be driven out and bound fast to a rock at the edge of the world, until the resurrected Kereshasp will come to annihilate him at the end of time.

Does it all sound familiar? Much of it is certainly reminiscent of the Gospel stories in Matthew: the mythically bloody tyrant Herod (certainly presented as dragonish in nature) who massacres innocent children, his plot to kill Jesus, the flight of the Holy Family into Egypt, etc. The association of Egypt with the Exile of the Jewish people with Moses and the wilderness-tradition makes a further strong parallel, suggesting in a similar way to the Iranian legend that after the period of exile there will be a return in triumph. The kingdom to which Jesus will lay claim, like the rule of Light in the Zoroastrian conception, is also an eternal or future one. Moreover, several events in the Gospel story involve learning things about the newborn Jesus in a dream. And there are odd features of the Gospel narrative, as when the visiting Magi see 'the young child and his mother Mary' (Matt.2:11), with Joseph strangely being forgotten despite his prominence throughout most of the Matthaean infancy chapters. Might we detect materials from a special source which focussed, as does the *Apocalypse of Adam* version, on the child and his mother? (In the original tale, remember, the father died.)

Altogether we have in these two stories, of Zal and Faridun, circulating among Jewish visionary movements which used *1 Enoch,* the Dead Sea Scrolls, the *Apocalypse of Adam,* etc., a startling number of the features exhibited in the Gospel story of Jesus! Consider:

There is the child begotten in uncertainty and anxiety over possible sin. Yet he is watched over by an angel (cf. Enoch, etc.), who reassures his father and communicates a special name for him, saying that he is favoured by God, and that he will play a great part in the future restoration of things (human and, perhaps, cosmic): — the Kereshasp-Zal story. Then, the child is persecuted by the worldly usurper-tyrant, representative of the dark power that temporarily has the ascendancy on earth. Learning in a prophetic dream of his birth, the child-slaughtering tyrant pursues his family. Mother and child flee into a desert place, whence the child will return to fulfil his destiny, though he is not the one to kill the king: — the Faridun story.

The *Apocalypse of Adam* places these two stories side by side in its sequence of birth-legends, and they appear within the document as part of a block of special material of this kind, indicating that it probably already belonged together before the work as a whole was composed and incorporated it. Might such a block of material be related to the traditions behind Matthew 1–2? It cannot be denied that the story-motifs are identical, and the way that they are employed in the Jewish visionary tradition would make sense of the Gospel's usage: they are used to bring out the deeper spiritual significance of a figure from the Bible, indicating a universal meaning that will reveal the total truth, including pagan ideas, in the light of the true God. One feature is the idea of coming at a turning-point, when the dark powers are apparently winning the day. At precisely such a time the new light-child is born. When it was said of such a figure that he had survived the massacre of the innocents, for instance, people would have understood that this meant escaping from the negative and corrupting, 'Ahrimanic' or dark influences which were outwardly prevalent — whether in the ruthless tyranny of a 'dragon king,' or in the wisdom of the 'fallen angels' that prevented knowledge of the true wisdom just mentioned. The stories applied to Jesus thus point to him as one who will possess the true esoteric wisdom that will reconcile all knowledge with religious truth in the new age that he inaugurates. Moreover, the wonder-child Jesus is destined, the stories indicate, to be a dragon-slayer. If that seems too pagan and mythological a notion, we need only turn to the Book of Revelation which ends the New Testament! Chapter 12 describes in an imaginative, 'visionary' way the birth of Jesus,

and at the same time tells of the 'great Dragon' lurking and waiting to get hold of him and his mother. The child is divinely protected, however, and 'caught up to God and his Throne.' A 'war in
heaven' between the Dragon and his angels, and the good angels,
with a reference to time-periods allotted to the Dark power, no
doubt symbolizes the turning-point of history at which Jesus
comes. Some scholars have argued that this story is actually the
same as appears in the *Apocalypse of Adam* — i.e. the Faridun-
story. That may be going beyond the evidence: but the passage
in Revelation certainly does demonstrate that people would have
recognized in Jesus one who is engaged from the moment of his
birth in a divinely aided struggle against the 'dragon' forces of
evil, and who will finally be vindicated by God.

And, last but not least, the Faridun-figure is born 'from a virgin
womb.' — Or is he? Just when we seem on the verge of tying a
legend with a virgin birth into the background of the Gospels we
meet still another frustration. For nothing of the sort is related
by Firdausi, or by the old Iranian sources. So where did the idea
come from in the *Apocalypse of Adam*? Fortunately, this question can be answered. For one of the earliest studies of the ideas
behind the *Apocalypse of Adam* showed that it has been influenced by details of the legend of the Saoshyant, the Zoroastrian
World-Saviour who was expected to be born in the last days to
bring about the Transfiguration of the earth. And he will be born
of a pure virgin. In fact, he is to be born of a virgin — more than
once.

Reincarnation!

It was mentioned previously that the Saoshyant is prophesied to
be born of a virgin. It was also mentioned he is in some sense
the completion and a sort of perfected reappearance of the original prophet Zarathustra. And, finally, it was mentioned that in
Zoroastrian thought human beings are asked constantly to renew
their commitment to the cause of Light and Truth by a series

of emissaries (sometimes translated 'Apostles') of the higher world and the God of Light, Ohrmazd — in a sense ever repeating the call of Zarathustra to perform good deeds, good words and good thoughts over the millennia of earthly history. The Zoroastrian mythology of the virgin birth is closely connected with these ideas, for it is the mythology of the 'posthumous sons' of Zarathustra.

Normally, one's children are a continuation of one's earthly existence through a family line. And Zarathustra had sons in the normal way. However, one's spiritual children are the reality of what comes from the good deeds, words and thoughts that one has set going in the world. And in the case of Zarathustra, these 'sons' will live on until the end of the world when the Saoshyant comes and embodies them definitively in his person — since his name and role actually come from the prophetic words of Zarathustra, 'Let righteousness be embodied.' That is one primary sense in which he will be virgin-born: his existence is not the result of ordinary human processes but of a prophetic word. Moreover, wherever the ideals of the Light are so embodied, the spirit of Zarathustra is, so to speak, present again and could be thought of as reincarnated in those 'emissary' figures who renew his message. Gradually, it seems, the Zoroastrian perspective prevailed and all the greatest heroes in the fight against the Dark, Ahrimanic principle came to be seen as partial embodiments of the spirit of Zarathustra. The Saoshyant is the last and greatest of these, but even he, as a scholar of Zoroastrianism has remarked, still appears wielding the mace of the ancient fighters and heroes.

As we have seen, each hero is born at a dark hour. In the Zoroastrian metaphysic, the struggle of the Light and Dark means that the conflict grows darker and more intense, until a new Light-hero comes to start a new cycle. In the traditional Zoroastrian account, there are three such ages after the age of Zarathustra himself, when he appeared as the great Teacher of the Light, the Illuminator. And for each age there has to be a renewal of the message of Light, for which a 'son' of Zarathustra will be born, who in reality is the spirit of the prophet appearing again. (Other versions of the legend give seven appearances, the last being the Saoshyant. And in less orthodox literature we hear of twelve figures, and of twelve cosmic ages.) In the mythological picture-language of Zoroastrianism, the process is described rather evocatively: As well as his ordinary sons, then, Zarathustra begot three posthumous sons. From his seed the creative 'power and light' was three times taken by the messenger-god (cf. angel, messenger) and hidden, awaiting the future, in the depths of a dark lake. At night, it was said, people peering into the depths could see the glowing points of light far below. And it will come about that once in each future age, when that cycle of time has reached the phase of dark struggle, a pure virgin will go to bathe in the lake and become with child. And she will give birth to a miracle-child who is the renewal of the Light-revelation, and a 'posthumous son,' i.e. reincarnation, of Zarathustra. The last of these, in the final age, will be the Saoshyant, the World-Saviour.

In the *Apocalypse of Adam,* we have a number of stories in the cycle of legends and myths about the Illuminator which contain explicit references to virgin birth, along with several related ideas (e.g. a goddess who gives birth to the wonder-child without impregnation, or another who desires to drink water from a magic flower and from it conceives the child, etc.). We also seem to have a very specific allusion to the Saoshyant mythology, as was immediately spotted by the expert in Iranian studies, Alexander Böhlig. He pointed out that the recurring phrase 'And thus he came on the water' reflects the underlying idea in the Saoshyant mythology of the child born from the waters of the lake, through the virgin who goes to bathe there. With the refrain in the *Apocalypse of Adam* goes a phrase about the child receiving Glory and power. The Saoshyant in Zoroastrian sources is said to be endowed once more with the divine Glory or radiance which belonged to the first man in paradise, but was afterwards forfeited by humanity for the archetypal sin in Zoroastrian eyes: the Ahrimanic deed of telling an untruth. This Glory was likewise said to have been preserved in the depths of the ocean since that terrible moment of humanity's fall. In fact, this conception of the submerged Glory and its reappearance from the waters in connection with an eschatological hero is probably the oldest element in the whole Saoshyant myth, since it occurs in various forms in Indo-European literature from India and elsewhere, as well as in ancient Iran.

Gradually, then, a mythological idea connected with the creative power hidden in the watery depths, associated with the unfallen world and with the end of time, was given a special prophetic meaning by Zoroastrianism. In the myths of older times, the divine Glory was already supposed to have reappeared to hover over the great heroes, such as Zal and Faridun, and give them supernatural power in the fight against the Dark forces. The idea of the hidden light appearing anew from the darkness came together with the Zoroastrian idea that all of human history was a version of one on-going struggle between the Light and the Dark, Ohrmazd and Ahriman. All the heroes who had 'borne the Glory' became embodiments of the spirit who had first made known that tremendous truth. Each was born as a light in a time of darkness. The Saoshyant was conceived as the final hero who would achieve the victory to which they had all contributed. The prophet Zarathustra was the teacher who had revealed to humankind the message of Light which made sense of it all.

In orthodox Zoroastrianism, the ancient heroes are no more than helpers of the main figures — Zarathustra, the Saoshyant. But we have seen too that there was a tendency for the 'posthumous sons' to multiply to three, to seven, or to twelve, belonging to the different times and places where the good fight was carried on in history. In the *Apocalypse of Adam* we find all of the symbolism: light and darkness; cycles of history represented by the twelve Kingdoms of the world, together with a final Thirteenth Kingdom when the struggle against the Darkness reaches its climax and brings in the last times; the Illuminator (Zarathustra) and a further series of twelve embodiments or incarnations, all heroes or prophets miraculously born, the last of whom is evidently the World Saviour. And the idea of miraculous virgin birth belonging to the Saoshyant is extended in a sort of theme-and-variations fashion to all the incarnations, since they are essentially anticipations of his great spiritual work, the bringing about of the Transfiguration. The generation of humanity who see that day themselves shine like stars.

Now, it is true that the stories concerning at least two of the heroes who came to be seen as stages in the twelvefold cycle of incarnations apparently underlie the stories in Matthew's infancy chapters. And it is clear that at least one of those hero-legends came to be associated with birth 'from a virgin womb,' through association with the final hero, the Saoshyant. But surely, many readers may object, conceptions such as these — reincarnation, cycles of time and cosmic rhythms, secret knowledge, supernatural Glory — surely these cannot possibly have been ideas known in the world to which the Gospels were addressed, which heard about the virgin birth of Jesus? It is all very well to suppose that narrative lines were taken over into visionary Jewish thought for their symbolic power. But could people in the devoutly Jewish community which obviously lies behind Matthew's Gospel really have thought in terms such as these?

The answer, however, once again seems to be yes. Not only could they, but they did. It is only in fairly recent scholarship that the world of Jewish Christianity has been reconstructed in careful detail and properly valued, as against the type of Christianity which was spread among the Gentiles by Paul and his fellow-workers. A travesty used to prevail in presentations of early Christian history, according to which the choice lay between an inward- and backward-looking 'Judaizing' trend, or the forward-looking and expansive tendency of the 'great Church.' But the truth is quite different. We have repeatedly noted that Judaism had universalistic aspirations, and was seeking for the deeper truth that would bring together all humankind, even before Christianity. Moreover, Paul was of course himself a Jew who certainly had no intention of leaving the Jews out of his conception of the universal *ekklesia*. Jewish Christianity tried in its own way to express the conviction that Jesus was the Messiah

— and came for all humankind. And it did so on the basis of the rather esoteric doctrines whose surface we have been assiduously scratching above, bringing them into a form that could be used to spread their conviction that in Jesus the hopes and ideals of humanity had been fulfilled.

Only recently have the fundamentals of Jewish Christianity been restored from the wreckage of ancient controversy and some of the Nag Hammadi texts. And they may prove surprising to many readers. One is a stress on the *feminine* aspect of God, understood as his Holy Spirit. (To this we shall return.) And the other is the concept of the reincarnating 'True Prophet,' whose final appearance as the Messiah or Christ heralds the fulfilment of the biblical promises.

Hippolytus of Rome reports on the views of a Jewish-Christian teacher, around the year AD 100: 'He asserts ... that Christ was not for the first time on earth when he was born of a virgin,' he says, but had been born many times. The fundamental idea of Christ he presented was of a reincarnating prophet, of whom it had been foretold that he 'would thus appear and exist among us from time to time, undergoing alterations of birth, and having his soul transferred from body to body' (*Refutation of Heresies* IX:12). Though this became 'heresy' to the Church, there is abundant evidence that it was a cornerstone of Jewish Christianity. Oscar Cullmann is an expert on the so-called 'Ebionite' theology of the later Jewish Christians, which held, as he says, exactly the same idea: 'Since the creation of the world, the True Prophet hastens through the centuries, changing his name and form of appearance. He incarnated himself again and again.' And for the Jewish Christians, 'Jesus is the true incarnation of this Prophet.' Nor was it just a later idea. The Jewish scholar David Flusser has found definite traces of the concept in the Gospels, and concluded that already in Jesus' lifetime some of his disciples must have seen in him a prophet of this type. And now the *Apocalypse of Adam* adds its testimony, also from around the turn of the era: for it is clear that in his final, thirteenth appearance the Illuminator is to be identified with the Messiah, or coming Christ. That must have been the striking feature of its teaching to those who read it at that time. The reappearing Teacher of Light, destined to be the future Saoshyant or World Saviour, is also to be the Messiah of Jewish prophetic hope: it is yet another statement of that belief among the visionary sects of Judaism that their religion of the true God and his Messiah will also be revealed as the key to all other religions and hopes in the coming new age.

Perhaps we begin to see how Jesus might be regarded as fulfilling the pattern of several past types (the 'Zal' type, the 'Faridun' type, etc.). Make what we will of the startling notion of his many previous lives, one thing is clear. The concept of the Messiah among the esoteric sects had been coloured by the World-Saviour ideal, the Saoshyant who sums up all the struggles of the past and will take the world forward into the new time, the Transfiguration. He brings together all the stories of the heroes of the Light. The Essenes and Jewish Christians also found such types intimated — for those who could see — in the stories of the Bible. The evangelist we know as Matthew shares some at least of their esoteric thought-world. For him Jesus' birth shows that he is a summation of previous patterns of the spiritual life, as manifested at turning points like those of the patriarchs or Noah the time of the Flood. And more than that: he is the ultimate fulfilment, the Greater One, the future world starting to reveal itself.

The virgin birth idea is somewhere at the heart of this amazing symbolism. But can we find out how it was understood by those who took the ideas over into the Jewish milieu? Indeed we can. To do so, however, we must meet a still further cast of characters, including Noah's rather less well-known brother, Nir; the ancient priest-king Melchisedek — and even the Queen of Sheba.

4. A Near Miss and the Wrong Virgin

Melchizedek

An early section in the Bible tells of Abraham taking sides in a local skirmish, and returning victorious after the kings of Sodom and Gomorrah have been routed. As he returns, there comes out to meet him, in a famous episode, Melchizedek the king of Salem, who gives him bread and wine in return for which the victor allots him a tenth-part share (tithe) of the spoils. Melchizedek is a king but also, it turns out, a priest of El Elyon — translated in traditional versions as God Most High: an epithet almost unknown in reference to the biblical God, but nowadays very familiar from the rediscovered literature of the ancient Near East, where it denotes the supreme divinity in the pantheon of the pagan Semitic peoples. Such a 'High God' was a typical feature of the religion of Babylonia too, where the cosmic divinity presides over the council of the deities who each govern aspects of human and earthly life.

You would never guess from this short episode in the Bible that Melchizedek is the subject of a whole history of fascinating interpretation. In the Jewish tradition, it may be surprising to discover, he is identified with Noah's son Shem; his city of Salem is identified with Jerusalem (as it will be called); and some basic principles of religious law are drawn from the tithing of the spoils for him as a priest, in which role he is usually interpreted to be one of Abraham's early 'converts.' In Christian tradition, notably in the letter called 'Hebrews' included with those of Paul in the New Testament, on the other hand, Melchizedek has become a completely mystical figure. He is 'without father, without mother;' his gesture of welcome to Abraham by giving bread and wine is likewise mystically,

or 'typologically' interpreted too — God brought it about, we
gather, as a subtle hint of the Christian eucharist to be celebrated in the far future. And Jesus, who could not have qualified as a properly descended Jewish priest, nevertheless holds
an exalted priestly office — 'after the order of Melchizedek.'
In fact, God has exalted him in an unprecedented way, making
him his 'son,' which not even the angels can claim. What has
happened in between?

It has been recently argued that there really was a
Melchizedekian priesthood in Judaism in the period of the
kings, later replaced by the priests who claimed descent from
Moses and Aaron. Many of the Psalms were evidently originally
used for the rites of enthronement and coronation of the kings,
and remained associated with King David. Certainly Psalm 110
seems to suggest that the kings claimed a priestly-religious
right as 'God's anointed' (christ):

> The Lord said to my Lord,
> Sit at my right hand, and I will make your enemies a foot-
>   stool beneath your feet! ...
> The Lord has sworn, and will not go back on his oath:
> You are a priest for ever, after the order of Melchizedek.

Margaret Barker has argued that the kings were much more
important as religious figures than the 'edited' version of biblical history preserved by the later priesthood allowed to show
through. Only later did the cult approximate to a form acceptable to the conceptions of later Judaism. Earlier on, the ideal of
the priest-king was potent, whereas the priestly tradition later
turned rather hostile to the kings. The priestly-royal charismatic
ideas might have survived however, she suggests, and Jesus
could have inherited them, as she claims early Christianity also
did in its liturgy and doctrine of atonement. She finds reappearing in the Church many traditions and secrets of this long suppressed ancient order. No doubt there were underground ideas
and survivals from older forms. But we must be sceptical of the

stubborn continuance of this supposed Temple-tradition, resurfacing in Christian times. Remember that early Christianity had no priests, but Christ's living presence was celebrated by charismatics, prophets and holy men; that the Temple was destroyed in AD 70 by the Romans in the bloody events of the Jewish Revolt, and the Christians undoubtedly benefited from their new kind of religion that was not tied to a holy place or a building: in Revelation's vision of the 'heavenly Jerusalem' which replaces the earthly one there is no Temple, because the Lord himself is present and shines upon all. It is hard to see this as reviving a priesthood.

What was the reality of 'Melchizedek'? It is a difficult question to answer. What we can say is that his name was used in almost talismanic fashion by some of those esoteric and visionary groups which we have so often found cause to mention. The Dead Sea Scrolls brought the discovery, in Cave 11 at Qumran, of a hitherto unknown writing about him. His exaltation has there reached hitherto unimaginable heights, so that he is hardly a human being at all, but a cosmic power. In Hebrew his name seems to suggest the interpretation 'King of Righteousness,' and in this role he is set by the Essenes opposite the 'King of Wickedness,' Melkiresha — the Ahrimanic power which is opposed to the Light in their Zoroastrian-influenced theology. Another work called *Melchizedek* was found at Nag Hammadi, and appears to be based on the ritual assimilation of an initiated person to the mystical figure of the patriarch. It is possible that it too has a Jewish background, even if it reflects Gnostic theology. For some Jewish mystical works speak about such a transformation into a quasi-divine being. Whether or not we can succeed in discovering the older sources of the Gnostic writing, the evidence overall is enough to point away from the historical, Jerusalem priesthood even in the period of the kings. What the visionary sects are doing is rather using 'Melchizedek' as a name for the power of divine-spiritual transformation associated rather closely with their own, esoteric line. It is they who aspired to become quasi-angelic beings, playing a part in the cosmic work of the transformation of the world like the angelic hierarchies who express God's power and creative will.

It is not historically preserved Temple-traditions that would naturally be represented by Melchizedek, who in the Bible, after all, long precedes the Temple and worships God under a name that was never associated with the priestly tradition. But he is a very natural figure to choose as representing that Mystery-interpretation which is found by the esotericists in the Bible, though it looks to the literalists more like the wisdom of the pagans. He runs parallel, so to speak, like the esoteric interpretation itself, but independent of the mainstream or literal following of the Bible, and the priestly cultus in Jerusalem which is the historical focus of Israel's worship. He has a lingering aura of paganism, as does his 'God Most High' — who is nevertheless acknowledged by Abraham, as is Melchizedek's priesthood by his award of the tithe. The esotericists did not break with Judaism, but believed it to be the true religion and the key to the future. Yet to be that it must contain the truth behind pagan wisdom too: and of that esoteric synthesis Melchizedek appears to be the most potent representation. To be united with Melchizedek in secret ritual would mean to attain the fullness of esoteric knowledge, to know the secret deeper side of the Bible's outward historical narrative, and to become part of the cosmic-creative power of the Light itself in its war against 'Melkiresha,' the spirit of Darkness. No wonder that his priesthood is 'for ever,' and that he is 'without father and mother' rather than a human being. Yet at the same time he appears enigmatically in biblical history and is coeval with Abraham himself — the historical beginning of the Jewish faith, the father of all the Jews.

It is not true to say, however, that he is simply beyond or above human parentage. For in some legendary versions he is assigned something that, if it is not strictly quite a virgin birth is such a near miss that many scholars of the work called 2 Enoch have considered it one. Indeed, they usually refused to believe that the story was really an old Jewish legend at all, and thought the passage had probably been reworked by Christians to foreshadow the virgin birth of Christ. In the light of the Dead Sea Scrolls and the Gnostic *Melchizedek,* however, it seems to most of them that it belongs to the process, which we have briefly traced, of Jewish elevation of Melchizedek into an esoteric symbol. Christ's 'Melchizedekian' priesthood/kingship, and his possibly related miraculous birth, thus takes on a more definite significance.

But there are more surprises in store. For when we meet *2 Enoch*'s Melchizedek he has slipped through a sort of hole in history back to the time of the Flood, before even Abraham. Yet he is not Noah's son Shem — though perhaps this odd tradition of the Rabbis was related to the esoteric ideas. He is connected with a person not, I think I may be confident in saying, generally known: Noah's brother, Nir.

A near miss

The character and origin of the 'Book of the Secrets of Enoch' (*2 Enoch*) has long eluded scholarly pigeon-holes. It survives only in a Slavonic translation, of uncertain date, having been used by the Slavonic Orthodox Church. So it made sense for scholars to be cautious about accepting its legend of Melchizedek's miraculous birth as authentically Jewish and ancient. Nowadays, however, in the light of the Dead Sea Scrolls, there is a new consensus that it is indeed from the time-period of the first century BC–first century AD. It has even been suggested that Jesus wrote it. (Not a very likely guess.) Its ideas seem to be unorthodox Jewish teachings on the one hand, with cosmological ideas and other, obscurer matters that come from Zoroastrianism. This mix is not dissimilar to that found in the Essene writings of the Scrolls generally — except that it is a less stable and religiously acceptable fusion. Whereas the Essenes became a major Jewish group, one of the three main parties alongside Sadducees and Pharisees, the group which used *2 Enoch* tends more in a proto-Gnostic direction.

One sign of that leaning is that the literal history and the esoteric interpretation, Abraham and Melchizedek, do not just run parallel, as the Essenes supposed: there is an apparent tendency to play one off against the other. There is a kind of rivalry for the prime place of importance. And hence, I shall suggest, the tensions in the story of Melchizedek are much exaggerated in comparison with the versions we have been studying so far. By assimilating the truth of the Mysteries, the Essenes felt basically that they were fulfilling the Bible's deeper truth, but also naturally experienced anxiety and some guilt that they might be forfeiting their Jewish identity, and violating the beliefs of ordinary Jews. In *2 Enoch's* story the cleavage cuts still deeper, and is dramatized in powerful symbols. Moreover the already numerous cast of the biblical history essentially has to be doubled by an otherwise unknown set of parallel, esoteric figures: not only Noah who saves humankind, in his own person and that of his sons, but also his mysterious brother Nir; not only the Melchizedek who met Abraham, but a prior Melchizedek (or whole series of Melchizedeks) at the very outset of history. The two traditions are not in easy harmony: the esoteric seems to be constantly overturning the literal and pushing for first place. It is not the Noah who outwardly preserves the human race who matters, so much as the miracle-child of his priestly-esoteric brother Nir. It is not so much the Melchizedek who greets Abraham who matters, so much as the 'true' original Melchizedek who stands behind him.

As a result, the birth-story concerning Melchizedek in chapter 71 is among the most strange, even bizarre, extreme, and striking, of all that I know among ancient legends (some of which are pretty strange).

Noah's brother Nir is an aged priest, married to a similarly ageing wife, Sopanim. She has long been past the age of child-bearing, and moreover he has not had relations with her since he took his priestly vow. They have therefore refrained from sex for 202 years. Imagine therefore her horror when she finds one day that she is pregnant. She keeps the fact secret from Nir, until the day comes for the birth of the child. Nir then unexpectedly summons her to the Temple, and she cannot conceal her condition. Nir is scandalized and ashamed, thinking she has committed a sin, and rebukes her. He tells her to go. She protests however that she does not know how the child in her womb has come to be conceived.

This was exactly the line of Mary in the *Protevangelium*. Moreover, the conception in old age, without there having been intercourse, is the story told in that same apocryphal work about the birth of Mary herself — the so-called 'immaculate conception.' And it recalls the story woven in by Luke with the story of Jesus' birth, namely the birth of John the Baptist from an aged priestly pair. But of course even more obviously it is a version of the scandal-and-rebuke-story, with the divinely-innocent pregnancy being misunderstood and thought sinful, that runs through from the Dead Sea Scrolls onwards. We expect at any moment an angel, or perhaps Enoch himself in his angelic persona, to give a visionary reassurance that all is well .... Instead, the symbolism is pushed to a startling further intensification. So innocently appalled is Sopanim at her husband's rebuke that — she falls down dead!

Now it is Nir's turn to be repentant. In his distress he protests to the Lord that he did not lay a hand upon her. Then he goes and pours out the whole terrible story to his brother Noah.

Noah comes back with him to the house, and after some discussion advises him to keep the whole affair secret. They will bury Sopanim immediately (not a suspicious procedure, of course, in a hot country where it is the norm). No-one will ever hear of her shameful pregnancy. (Remember in the Gospel of Matthew how Joseph muses that he might send Mary away secretly to avoid public disgrace.) They dress Sopanim in black garments and lay her on the bed, and go to dig the grave in secret. But their plan is disrupted by the events which follow. For while they were away the child in the dead Sopanim's womb came out alive. When they come back they find him sitting upright on the bed beside his mother, already fully developed like a three-year-old, having wrapped himself in her clothing. And immediately he spoke: 'He opened his lips and blessed the Lord.'

At first Noah and Nir are simply terrified out of their wits. But his words of blessing make them think that God is renewing the priesthood 'according to his good pleasure.' They dress the child in priestly garments, and give him consecrated bread to eat. They bury Sopanim, not now in black but in bright garments, and the three of them build a shrine to her memory. And they call the child Melchizedek.

Noah next advises Nir to keep the child at home and mention him to no-one. For, he says, the people in all the earth are becoming sinful, and if they get to know about him they will come and kill him. For they are totally ignorant of the true God. His estimate of humanity is soon proved to be true, and humankind becomes increasingly lawless, so that Nir is filled with worries about the child whom he keeps all the while secretly in his home. He prays to the Lord to reveal to him the meaning of the child and his destiny. God then appears to him in a dream, a 'vision of the night,' and explains that he is about to overwhelm sinful humankind in a great catastrophe.

We are now back on the tracks of the familiar storyline. The miracle-child is born in a time of the prevalence of darkness and sin; even his father is agonized in soul over the strange child who has been born to him; the infant must escape from the threat of death from the uncomprehending world; dream-visions guide his father; etc. Moreover, God now explains that the child points to the future and the renewal of humanity and the (priestly) worship of the true God, again much as in the Noah-legend of the Dead Sea Scrolls and *1 Enoch*. The child's apparently dark and sinful origins point, for those who can discern these things, to his mission of renewing the light.

Except that in this version, no-one can discern it, with the exception of Noah and Nir themselves. For the author of *2 Enoch*, the deeper truth embodied in the wonder-child is completely esoteric, and cannot be entrusted to external humanity at all. The wonder-child is known about, literally, only in the priestly home, and is otherwise utterly hidden from the world. Nor does he ever become known, since (as God explains) Melchizedek is to be caught up to Paradise by the angel who will shortly come for him, and there remain until after the Flood. In due course the time will come for another Melchizedek, 'in the style of this Melchizedek,' who has been in hiding for seven years so that he does not get killed, to come out and encounter Abraham.

In external terms, the narrative is extraordinarily self-defeating. Completely defying the historical framework of the Bible while leaving it strangely intact, the legend adds a whole secondary set of parallel characters, but then ensures that what it has added remains completely and utterly hidden and removed from the known and recorded events. Melchizedek is made to be miraculously born long before the occurrences in which he figures in the Bible. Yet the story makes him be born, only to live in complete confinement; and be rescued, only so that he can be carried over to a later time by the angel, when he will perform his familiar role. For what purpose has the author created this utterly inconsequential sequence?

First of all, we may remind ourselves of the pattern of the story. Though almost every feature of it is exaggerated and intensified, it is really the same story we found applied to Noah in the Scrolls and *1 Enoch*. It is the Zal-story. The child when he is born fills his father with anxiety and the belief that he is a sinful product of the evil powers. The father rejects him (in this case while he is still in his mother's womb). The child however is under the protection of the magic/divine-angelic being (Simurgh, angel, Enoch). In the original myth the child is taken off to the magic mountain or Paradise at the ends of the earth, or in later versions his father (or his deputed representative) has to travel to the mountain to get the reassuring oracle or, in effect, to get the child whom he has rejected back. In *2 Enoch* the child is carried off to Paradise by an angel, whose original identity is unknown because some texts call him Michael, others Gabriel. The fact that he is taken up on wings is much stressed (whereas ancient angels rarely have wings). As well as indicating that the Paradise to which he goes is on a mountain above the level of the Flood, it is surely a reminiscence of the prototype magic bird (Simurgh). He does return to earth, but the story again violently breaks the narrative line by making him do so only to bring out of hiding another version of Melchizedek — the one who historically came to meet Abraham. The father Nir does in a way get his son back, so to speak, when the oracle about the angel reveals to him the future destiny of the child, as in all the versions. But in this instance, Nir also thereby loses the child to the future, and since he has no other son the reaction stressed by the author is simultaneous 'joy and grief.' Although the wonder-child has been born to continue the priesthood of the true God, when Nir dies the priesthood ceases — so that the basic story-symbolism is turned on its head yet again. A story fundamentally about renewal becomes that of the end of the line. A story about new hope becomes one of the coming of chaos: 'After him there was no priest among the people. And from that time great confusion arose on the earth' (ch.72). What could one expect from a child whose birth was a death?

This version of the story seems to be challenging our whole set of assumptions, at least if we suppose that renewal is about some sort of continuity into the future. External history, as represented in the story of Noah, shows us the survival of (good) humanity because one man and his family are rescued and provide continuity. The Bible is largely in accord with this historical idea of continuity; Israel is God's people because it has remained faithful throughout history and still upholds the tradition today. The story in *2 Enoch* does not deny the reality or the importance of this outward continuity: the future Melchizedek will emerge from his cave on the mountain of Ararat where the ark of Noah rests. But it makes a very strong point that outward continuity is not enough to ensure the handing on of spiritual reality and truth. The outer history contained in the Bible, it implies, is not the whole picture. The inner meaning of what it has to tell has to be rediscovered ever and anew. The esoteric meaning cannot be communicated in external terms, or handed down through outward perpetuation of a people or a tradition. Hence the basic picture of death as well as birth. But we should not despair, because the esoteric meaning, the higher truth behind the outer history, is always there in the eternal, magic realm of Paradise above the waves of time and calamity. It will be found again by those who are waiting, so to speak, ripening, ready to recognize it when it descends from heaven, to find an earthly reflection once more.

The basic symbolism may start to make some sense in this light. The mysterious, totally esoteric Melchizedek who is born before the Flood is an indication of the way that, for the author of *2 Enoch,* an event like the meeting of Melchizedek with Abraham is the reappearance, the manifestation, of the spiritual truth that has been grasped from time immemorial by those who were able to penetrate behind the outer surface of history. But it has never been known — or has been secretly feared and hated — by ordinary humanity. It is the eternal truth that is treasured in Paradise by the angels. It is also known to those worthy of it on earth, but their knowledge is not handed down externally. They form rather a mystic sequence quite distinct from the Bible's outward history. Thus we learn that the Melchizedek who is born so secretly is the 'head,' that is, the climax, of a whole series of twelve priests 'who existed before' — reaching back to primordial times, all before the Flood. Melchizedek will reappear after the Flood to bring the esoteric knowledge once more to his physical successor, or next incarnation as we might say. And then, we are told, 'there will be another Melchizedek, the first of twelve great priests,' all to come, after the Flood. And the last, or thirteenth who follows them all, will be the greatest, the 'head of all,' called in some texts 'the Word and Power of God.' Perhaps that is a Christian interpolation: but it is based on what is obviously a right understanding of the text. For we may recognize on the one hand the similarity of these doctrines to the Zoroastrian idea of the (three, seven or twelve) reincarnations of the Saoshyant, the World-Saviour; and on the other, the background of the Jewish-Christian teachings about the True Prophet, whose last incarnation they considered to be Jesus.

An intermediate stage, between the Zoroastrian and the Jewish or Jewish-Christian teaching, is found in the twelve incarnations of the Illuminator in the *Apocalypse of Adam.* There too the thirteenth will be the Messiah. And the account

of history (outward and esoteric) given by that document confirms the interpretation of the Melchizedek figure. Not that
Melchizedek is mentioned by name, but esoteric insight is associated with a spiritual race, whose presence runs parallel or is
interwoven with that of Noah and his sons who on the external
level inherit the earth after the Flood. Alongside the Noachic
progeny there also appear the bearers of this secret wisdom
'who were sent forth from the knowledge of the great aeons and
the angels.' When their earthly existence is threatened, moreover, angelic beings 'will come down to take those men out of
the fire and the wrath and bring them above the aeons ... [their]
dwelling-place ... [will be] with the holy angels and the aeons.
The men will resemble those angels, for they are not strangers
to them.' The place to which they are caught up is probably
the angelic Paradise. We have the same picture as in 2 *Enoch*.
When the esoteric knowledge is threatened by erring humanity,
it disappears but is taken up to Paradise, to reappear again in a
new cycle, being born to manifest itself ever and anew in secret
among those who can understand it, a 'spiritual race.' Thus
we have a Fourteenth view of the Illuminator too, which is the
vantage of eternal truth. But it does not mean another kingdom
on earth after the incarnation as the Messiah: it is the deeper
Jewish-esoteric truth that complements and reveals the deeper
meaning in the biblical promise of the Messiah's coming.

The Melchizedek-story shows a highly esoteric version of
ideas which we know from other documents related to the Gospel
of Matthew, such as *1 Enoch* and the *Genesis Apocryphon* on
Noah. New emphasis is also placed on the secret rhythms
of the inner, secret manifestation — or miraculous birth: the
twelve representative figures in each cycle, before and after the
Flood. Such ideas must already have guided the other versions
when they looked for a suitable Jewish 'equivalent' story and
found Noah, whose importance at the critical time of the Flood
we now see makes him the obvious figure to focus upon. The
Flood ends a phase of world-history; but the story is to tell how
esoteric knowledge overleaps that ending, that catastrophe, and

will reappear — either as the deeper meaning of Noah himself (brought out by ascribing to him miraculous birth-stories) or through a parallel, highly esoteric doublet of Noah who is associated with the birth of the miracle-child Melchizedek. In Matthew, we recall, the Flood is likewise a 'type' of the coming of the Messianic time. Jesus too can be ascribed birth-stories which mark him out as one with a destiny like Noah or Melchizedek. In him also esoteric knowledge will be reborn, a new age will begin. That is why his birth is a miracle, is life from death, a secret light shining in a dark world.

And that is why a Jewish-esoteric adaptation of the story of a strange child, Zal (rejected by his father, associated with dark secrets but vindicated as a true child of light, in the meantime carried up to a mountain Paradise by a magic bird, and returning to the world to fight dragons), could be applied to several figures — not least of them, Jesus. Something very close to a virgin birth had already been ascribed to him, in connection with ideas of rebirth deriving from the Saoshyant-conception, in *2 Enoch*'s version of the tale, where he is Melchizedek. A virgin birth is ascribed in the *Apocalypse of Adam* to Faridun in its version of a story closely linked to that of Zal. We are finally closing in on the stories that make sense of the virgin birth in its Gospel-setting. And we may sense that the weird version of Melchizedek in *2 Enoch* is finally a genuine contribution to the background of Christianity. For the Christian message too will not be just about continuity, or God's people finally being brought home and rewarded: it will also involve suffering, crisis, apparent defeat and utter ending, out of which spiritual victory can nevertheless emerge. Something profoundly Christian is foreshadowed in that birth-out-of-death.

But to complete the backdrop to the infancy narratives of Matthew's Gospel we need to look at the story which follows immediately after these two in the *Apocalypse,* again involving a virgin birth. It is time to meet Solomon and the Queen of Sheba.

Arrival of the Queen of Sheba

Royal arrivals are almost invariably delayed for one reason or another. This gives us time to recapitulate briefly on the document called the *Apocalypse of Adam*. Though it was used by Christian Gnostics and discovered in a Gnostic library at Nag Hammadi, it is Jewish in form and in much of its content: it belongs in the tradition of visionary or esoteric Judaism of the time around Christian beginnings, when a new synthesis seemed possible and a new period was seen to be dawning in human-kind's religious history. Influences from Iran (the struggle of Light and Darkness) and from the Mysteries (rites of spiritual regeneration) were particularly important. Christianity is the heir to that sense of a breakthrough and spiritual renewal, and Jesus became the focus for many of these ideas, but much of its back-ground already lies in the astonishing literature of the Essenes and other Jewish visionaries at the time. Much that seemed hard to understand in early Christianity can now be grasped once more because of the important discoveries that have recently restored their works to us.

The *Apocalypse of Adam* is a vision from before the Flood (or so it claims) looking forward through history, following humankind's fall, the rescue of the 'spiritual race,' and extend-ing even to the Last Days. Many Jewish writings use this form, being attributed to archaic figures such as Enoch or Elijah. It is a way of trying to see history whole, from a great turning-point in the past, and so divine the meaning of the future. Crucial to the version of the past and future in the *Apocalypse of Adam* is the mission of the Illuminator. He is clearly modelled on the Iranian Saoshyant, the spiritual successor or rather reappearance of the great prophet Zarathustra. The legends told about him are all birth-legends, prophetically indicating his deeper nature, and point to his appearances in various kingdoms of the world throughout history, leading up to his final coming as the World Saviour. This, we may infer, is still in the future for the writer of the *Apocalypse.* The legends are held together by allusions to the idea which is known to have been central to the doctrine of the Saoshyant, namely miraculous birth from the spiritual seed of Zarathustra through a pure virgin.

Some of these legends, we have discovered, also left traces in the writings from the Dead Sea Scrolls and in the apocryphal books of Enoch (*1* and *2 Enoch*). What is perhaps most remarkable, however, is that so many of the relevant stories and ideas that link these writings to the stories told in the infancy chapters of Matthew's Gospel are all found together in a single block of material in the *Apocalypse of Adam* (V 76:26–79:19). The four stories it tells about the Illuminator contain extraordinary similarities to the stories woven together in the Gospel around the birth of Jesus. The First Kingdom tells of the birth of the Illuminator, who was of divine origin ('he was nurtured in the heavens') but who came down to 'the bosom of his mother' to be born, himself a revelation of the Light. The Second Kingdom tells the story of the ancient Iranian hero Zal: initially rejected by his father who thinks his mother has had contact with dark and sinful forces, he is nevertheless watched over by a magic being, the Simurgh, from whom his father subsequently learns that the child is a truly begotten, and destined to be a great fighter for the Light. The Third Kingdom tells another legendary story, that of Faridun: the child is the true heir to the throne usurped by the dragon-king, Azidahak; though just an infant, he is pursued by the murderous tyrant, and his family have to flee with the child from the city where they dwell; later Faridun will return to claim his throne, although the final blow against Azidahak cannot be dealt until the Last Days.

The Fourth Kingdom then tells a further story. It contains a more than one virgin as well as a virgin birth, and features King Solomon. It is not very straightforward however, and it is rather hard to keep track of the virgins. We need to examine it carefully, and to see whether it too may be related to the traditions behind the Gospel of Matthew.

The Fourth Kingdom says of him that he came from a
virgin [...]

Solomon sought her, he and Phersalo and Sauel and his ar-
mies which he had sent out. Solomon also sent out his army
of demons to seek the virgin.

And they did not find the one they sought; but the virgin
who was given to them was the one they brought.

And Solomon took her.

But the virgin conceived and gave birth to a child. She nurtured him on the borders of the desert. When he had been
nourished, he received Glory and Power from the seed from
which he had been begotten.

And thus he came on the water.

The story may not be instantly recognizable as an allusion to
1 Kings 10:1–15, where the Queen of the South comes to visit
Solomon and acknowledge his wisdom — but that is because it
is evidently based also on the legendary versions which grew up
around the event. Or possibly, since most of these are rather late,
the legendary versions reflect a telling of the tale like that in the
Apocalypse. Legendary versions are contained in the *Qur'an,* in
the semi-historical chronicles of the kings of Ethiopia, or *Kebra
Nagast,* and in oral tradition; almost all of them were collected by
Wallace Budge in his study and translation of what were at that
point all the relevant texts.

Nearly every feature of the *Apocalypse of Adam*'s story can be
paralleled when we take these into account. For instance, several
versions agree that 'Solomon sought her' — with the King initiat-
ing the contact with the Queen of the South rather than the other
way around; many of the legends make much of the involvement
of Solomon's army of demons; several of them also have a good

deal to say about the King's seduction of the virgin Queen, and the fact that Solomon begot on her a marvellous child, Menyelek; several of them (especially the oral versions) involve look-alikes and two women, with confusion of identity between their sons if not between the two women themselves, though none has precisely the story of substitution that we find here. There is enough similarity, in short, to assure us that the *Apocalypse of Adam* is basically following some handing-down of the story which we know from the legends and chronicles of later times. Unique to our version is the fact that though Solomon seduces a virgin, she is not the virgin Queen of Sheba (Ethiopia); nevertheless the virgin Queen returns to her Ethiopian homeland on the borders of the southern desert, and there gives birth, miraculously, virginally, to Solomon's truly-begotten son. (In some versions, the other woman also bears Solomon's son, who looks outwardly like his father but has not his princely-charismatic qualities.)

The story in all the legendary versions has so little to do with the original episode in the First Book of Kings that we must inevitably ask how it took on its present shape. Without going into details, it may be noted that (as I have argued elsewhere) the themes of look-alikes and recognizing the true prince by his royal charisma in the Menyelek stories has much in common with a famous story from Persian 'history' — the story of the accession of Darius. The customary version tells how a look-alike impostor had usurped the throne, but that Darius replaced him as the true heir of the Achaemenid dynasty. Some historians still accept the tale as a true account of what took place, but others find that it is implausible and full of mythic and fairy-tale motifs. Moreover, Darius constantly stressed his quasi-divine origins, using mythological language from several of the territories he conquered to assert his divine right, and in Iran presented himself with his six noble companions as if he were the living reflection on earth of Ohrmazd, the God of Light, with his six creator spirits, the Bounteous Immortals. It seems more likely that the tale of his look-alike echoes a royal-mythology, intimating the divine birth of the true king. A story somewhat like it, at any rate, seems to have fused with Ethiopian traditions and biblical reminiscences to produce the 'dualistic,' Zoroastrianized tale we find in the *Apocalypse of Adam*.

Such contact with Persian themes of dualism would also account for the way that Menyelek has come to be regarded as one in the sequence of embodiments of the Saoshyant prior to his climactic and final appearance as World Saviour. As such he also inherits the theme of virgin birth.

At least two of the stories in the preceding sequence of stories about the Illuminator are echoed, in precise narrative detail, in the account concerning Jesus in Matthew's Gospel. Whether or not David Flusser is right in finding traces of reincarnation-ideas in Matthew, Jesus evidently sums up all other religious manifestations and fulfils their partial ideal, and the stories applied severally to the heroes of the *Apocalypse of Adam* are all regarded as fulfilled by Jesus. So: Do we find there any trace of the story about Solomon and the virgin Queen? Apart from the virgin birth itself nothing is immediately obvious. There is no look-alike Jesus, no mistake about the identity of the virgin Mary.

There is, however, a constant theme that has touched several anxious nerves — the double aspect of Jewish and pagan in the stories, with the danger that was clearly felt of avoiding a slip back into paganism. The pagan truth had to be thoroughly transposed into the higher key of the new teaching for the future. And in Matthew's Gospel there is similarly a subtle but profoundly important doubling: there is certainly a Jewish Jesus, but there is definitely also a pagan Jesus — the Jesus who is known to the Gentiles coming into his church. Matthew clearly shares the universalism of Jewish Christianity, and we have mentioned already that the account of the coming of the Magi must have seemed to many at the time a gesture of reaching out to the pagan religious world. To see what is happening, we need to ask help from those scholars who have studied the actual text of the Gospel rather minutely.

Pulling at the seams: the text of Matthew 1–2

The Gospels have been subjected to an extraordinarily intensive analysis for something like two hundred years now. Literally every word has been studied, analysed and interpreted. As tends to happen when something is studied intensively, the result is that there are more and more conflicting conclusions.

Disagreements there certainly are over the infancy chapters of Matthew's Gospel. For some, they were simply written by the evangelist as a poetic expression of his theological views. Scholars point out that the Greek is thoroughly in Matthew's style, and we saw earlier that attempts to find in the content direct reminiscences from the family of Jesus collapse upon close inspection. On the other hand, to others it seemed hard to accept that an evangelist would feel free simply to invent stories about Jesus. Matthew has written his Gospel in his own words. But throughout he is obviously dependent upon the tradition of the Christian message about Jesus as it was taught orally, preached and handed on in the earliest communities. We cannot deduce from his hand in the style that the content was not traditional.

A more subtle analysis finds Matthew adapting already traditional materials to his stylistic and theological purpose. In fact his hand is rather easily detectable at certain moments: we saw earlier how he intervenes to prevent any misunderstanding about Mary's pregnancy — it was 'by the Holy Spirit,' he exclaims. With the exception of Luke's, the Gospels are not marked by literary finesse. Once we start to examine Matthew's narrative technique we soon find that there are apparent seams and joinings, and it emerges that several kinds of material have been used even in the opening chapters. On the whole the quest for the sources of the Gospels (such as the fictive 'Q') has been of questionable value. But the infancy chapters are surprisingly receptive to such an analysis, and I am pleased to record in defiance of my scepticism that extremely interesting results have been obtained from the 'literary' investigation of their composition, notably by the great Catholic scholar Raymond Brown.

One kind of interesting feature is the detection of strongly patterned narrative. Three times in chapters 1–2 there is an angelic dream-revelation to Joseph (1:20–5, 2:13–15, 2:19–21), and each time it is described in almost identical literary terms. Each time it begins with a clause setting the scene; then it mentions the dream-revelation; then the angel gives a command; the command is each time followed by an explanation of why it is given; and each time it is said that Joseph 'got up' and did what the angel told him. Angelic appearances in a dream do not appear anywhere else in the Gospel, and indeed an angel of the Lord appears only once more, in a resurrection setting. It is hard not to think that Matthew is incorporating a distinctive block of traditional, highly patterned story into his narrative. If we accept this, we may suppose that (unless Matthew was doing unexpected things with tradition), the situations to which the dream-revelations refer must have constituted parts of the story. Accordingly, Brown separates out the segments of the story which include or are mentioned in the angelic dream-visions.

He obtains a narrative-block with the following elements. An angel appears to the betrothed Joseph, telling him that Mary his wife will give birth to a son, who will save his people from their sins. Joseph takes her into his home as he is commanded, and Jesus is born in the days of King Herod. Herod learns of Jesus' birth (Brown speculates that this too would have been in a dream), and seeks him out, slaughtering all the children of similar age. But Joseph is warned in a dream to flee with the child and his mother into Egypt. He does so and stays there until the danger is past. Then the angel appears to him again in a dream and instructs him to return to Israel.

The resulting story is coherent, complete in the Gospel as it stands (except for the speculative mention of a dream of Herod), and marked by characteristic and unrecurring language (especially *kat' onar*, 'in a dream') and formalized narrative structures. But perhaps more startling is the fact that it corresponds spectacularly well with the narrative outline of the 'Third Kingdom' in the *Apocalypse of Adam* — the story, that is, of Faridun: the hero-child oppressed by the dragon-king, his mother fleeing with him from the city where they dwell, his being reared in exile, in the 'wilderness,' and returning to claim his kingdom. Interestingly, too, in Firdausi's recounting of the story, the dragon-king Azidahak learns of the existence of his young rival in a dream ...

Strikingly absent from the material thus linked together, on the other hand, is the scene of Mary's unexpected pregnancy and Joseph's agonized feelings, and the message of reassurance (quite different from the typical *command* given by the angel in the structured sequence of the above story). In other words, absent from the patterned block of narrative are precisely those elements that belong to the Zal story which we have found existing as a separate legend, told by the 'Second Kingdom' in the *Apocalypse of Adam* and told in the Dead Sea Scrolls about Noah, etc. Literary analysis of the Gospel thus confirms what we supposed, that the birth of Jesus is regarded as conforming to the pattern of several legendary 'types,' already thought of in connection with a coming World-Saviour, whose stories are fused together to indicate the several aspects of Jesus' all-fulfilling future destiny. The Zal-story which makes him a disturbing but ultimately creative wonder-child has been (not too deftly) dovetailed with the Faridun-story, which makes him a hero and dragon-slayer, oppressed in his childhood but ultimately granted victory by God.

Absent too from the patterned material is the story of the coming of the Magi. Various oddities and discrepancies were noted here too: Herod needs to know where the child is to be found, and sends his agents of destruction; however, they seem unable to follow the Magi or to know where they went to visit the holy family. Once more it is likely that an originally separate story has been brought into the complex. With fine intuition, J.E. Bruns noted that the visit of the Magi — pagan wonderworkers and priests — appears to be modelled on the story of the Queen of Sheba episode. According to 1 Kings 10 she brought with her gifts:

gold, aromatic spices and precious stones. Isaiah 60:6 echoes the scene, prophesying 'those from Sheba will come bringing gold and frankincense.' The legendary versions, especially the *Qur'an,* place great emphasis on the fact that Solomon gave her in return the knowledge of the true God.

We now know that the story of Solomon and the Queen had been adapted to a cycle of prophecies concerning the Illuminator-figure. And that, in turn, Jewish Christianity saw in Jesus the climactic fulfilment of such a series of prophets, the incarnations of the one True Prophet. The *Apocalypse of Adam* contains the sequence, and in some of the later oriental legends about the Magi there are further hints of the connection. The child who was born, virginally, to the Queen was a forerunner or prototype of the World-Saviour, and Matthew's Gospel (12:42) mentions the coming of the Queen as a sign of fulfilment. It is not surprising therefore that the infancy chapters indicate that the pattern of his birth was also realized in that of Jesus.

'My mother the Holy Spirit'

We are thus in a position to draw some conclusions about the virgin birth, at least as it features in the Gospel of Matthew. Matthew evidently comes from a Jewish Christian background, and he has points of contact with the visionary-esoteric sects of Judaism like the Essenes, which we now know to have produced a considerable literature. His stories of the birth and infancy of Jesus would have been readily understood among these sects, and also more widely because their ideas were popularized through the use of 'romance' forms such as *Joseph and Aseneth* — a typical piece of edifying imaginative literature with a deeper meaning for those who wished to pursue it. On a more esoteric level, a work like the *Apocalypse of Adam* shows how the expectation of the Messiah had become involved with the idea of a coming universal revelation. The Gentiles would also find their hopes fulfilled and their wisdom realized. Alongside the Bible's history of salvation, the esoteric sects came to believe in a continuous revelation of the deeper meaning that lay behind the Bible, which had been taught in secret throughout the ages, and which would enable all this to be explained. The nurturing of that spiritual truth through the ages, waiting and preparing for the great age that would finally dawn, was expressed in the idea of an Illuminator-figure, the Light-bringer, the True Prophet, appearing again and again through history. The Messiah was regarded as being the climactic and last appearance of his spirit, leading to a new spiritual world order, with the overcoming of the Darkness of ignorance and evil at last.

Several of the legends relating to such a figure have left their traces in the writings of the Dead Sea Scrolls, and in the Enochic literature. In them we find remarkably close analogies to the plots of the stories woven together in Matthew 1–2. But they do not contain the crucial motif of virgin birth. This motif comes into the stories specifically from the influential Zoroastrian prophecy of the Saoshyant: the great World Saviour who will be born from the 'spiritual seed' of Zarathustra when a pure virgin comes to bathe in the lake where it lies concealed. It is difficult to resist the conclusion of David Flusser, therefore, that the Gospel of Matthew itself alludes to the True Prophet idea, spelled out in later Jewish Christian literature. The virgin birth would signify that Jesus completes the cycle, and identifies him as the fulfilment of all humanity's hopes for a new and Light-filled world. Flusser considers that in the Enoch-literature the twelve priests after the Flood who stem from Melchizedek also represent twelve incarnations before that of the Messiah — not an outward priesthood, but an esoteric sequence parallel to the historical, specifically Jewish revelation. Whatever we make of the reincarnations, our researches have certainly confirmed that it is precisely these stories which have been utilized in Matthew to characterize the new-born Jesus as one destined to bring a new and universal revelation. The fact that four stories which come together in the *Apocalypse of Adam* are so closely connected with Matthew 1–2 again rather suggests that the completed *cycle,* and not just the individual motifs and legends, underlay the tradition Matthew used.

The aspect hardest to readjust to, for many, perhaps, is that the virgin birth in Matthew evidently has nothing whatever to do with the idea of Jesus as the Son of God. We have dealt already with the mistaken assumptions often brought to the citation of Isaiah 7:14. There is much evidence, too, that the earliest Christians did not assume that virgin birth meant divine Sonship. For example, an early Gnostic group asserted that divine Wisdom 'arranged the emanation of two men, one from the barren Elizabeth, the other from Mary the virgin ... Jesus, being born from a virgin by divine working, was wiser and purer and more just than all men' — but it was only afterwards that the Christ descended upon him, 'and so Jesus Christ came to be' (Irenaeus, *Against Heresies* I,30,12). In the eyes of the Jewish Christians likewise, it was at the baptism, not at birth, that Jesus became the Christ. In the Jewish Christian Gospel (the so-called *Gospel of the Hebrews* which was somehow closely connected to Matthew), the words of the Holy Spirit at the baptism of Jesus alluded to his prehistory as the True Prophet:

> And it came to pass that when the Lord was come up from
> the water, the whole fount of the Holy Spirit descended
> upon him and rested upon him and said to him: My Son, in
> all the prophets I was waiting for thee, that thou shouldest
> come and I might rest in thee. For thou art my rest; thou art
> my beloved Son, whose reign is for ever.

Later in that *Gospel,* too, Jesus speaks of 'my Mother the Holy Spirit' — the mother, that is to say, of his divine birth at the baptism.

There is nothing in Matthew's allusions to the Holy Spirit which require us to go beyond this Jewish Christian conception. The angel's reassuring reference to the offspring in Mary's womb in Matthew 1:20, many scholars have realized, does not require a capitalized divine Person at all. As we noted previously, it describes the child as a gift of God in a familiar Jewish sense: 'That which is begotten in her is from a spirit which is holy,' the angel explains, as opposed to the sinful and fallen spiritual influence Joseph apparently feared. The Matthaean intrusion, attributing Mary's pregnancy to the Holy Spirit, is to be understood in the sense indicated by the *Gospel of Hebrews* or similarly by the pre-orthodox Gnostic passage: the birth of Jesus is a providence of the Holy Spirit, a step in bringing about the fulfilment of the ages of waiting and prophesying, watched over by divine Wisdom. The virgin birth is a sign of the True Prophet, the Christ-bearer as he will be: but it is only later between baptism and resurrection that he will become 'Jesus Christ,' and as God's Son bring about something greater than even his extraordinary, legend-laden birth could predict.

5. The Christmas Gospel

Luke: The new paradigm

Our researches from an esoteric background, showing the reappearance of themes from Essene and Therapeutic writings in the infancy chapters of Matthew, have coincided remarkably with the literary analysis of the Gospel by a great Catholic theologian. Raymond Brown had concluded that at least three separate strands of tradition were joined together there: a highly patterned story about the dangerous situation of the child and his family, with repeated, even formulaic instructions given by angels in a vision, corresponding to our Faridun-story; a story of a nativity, also involving an angel but with a different kind of message, one of reassurance and prophetic promise, corresponding to our Zal-story; and a visit from pagan prophet-priests, modelled on and corresponding to our story of the Queen of Sheba (and her wonder-child). The correspondence is indeed remarkable. But there are a number of concrete differences (not surprising when we move from analysis and conjectural sources to real ones) which also call for comment. In fact, there are subtle discrepancies which must lead us to call in doubt many of the more far-reaching further conclusions of the Catholic scholar.

Brown is struck by the several points of contact between Matthew's story of the nativity and Luke's, in spite of the more obviously apparent divergences in their accounts. In both Gospels Mary and Joseph are a newly married couple;* in both Mary is unexpectedly found to be with child, a fact confirmed

---

* Non-Jewish readers have been confused by the circumstances of Mary and Joseph for at least two thousand years. The angel in Matthew 1:20 for instance calls her Joseph's wife, though the word earlier used for them is

or announced by an angel; the angelic annunciation reveals the divine-prophetic significance of the humanly unexpected event; the birth is (by inference) in both cases a virgin birth.

But is it?

As a matter of fact it has become clear that the story which provides the plot of the 'annunciation' did not include a virgin birth. The Zal-story is that of a disturbing child, who turns out to be salvific rather than demonic, divinely singled out rather than an offspring of sin. But in the Dead Sea Scrolls recension and in its parallel in *1 Enoch,* where it applies to Noah, Enoch is able to give an 'angelic' reassurance that the child is truly begotten. In the 'Second Kingdom' narrative in the *Apocalypse of Adam,* briefly outlining the whole tale, there is no mention of a virgin birth either — though it is explicitly recorded for the Third and Fourth Kingdoms, whose stories are also reflected in Matthew 1–2; it is therefore unlikely to be an oversight. Nor is virgin birth quite mentioned in the 'near miss' version, that of the birth of

---

normally translated 'betrothed.' But Mary is apparently not living with him, and they have clearly not had marital relations. The Gospel manuscripts show a rash of alterations as scribes tried to make sense of the situation, though a slight knowledge of Jewish marriage-customs soon makes all straightforward. Marriage, according to the Rabbis, is legally effected by an exchange of vows between the couple before witnesses, usually when the bride is about thirteen years old. It is this mutual 'consent' which constitutes the marriage. Thus it is really quite misleading to speak of 'betrothal,' which implies to us that there had been less than full personal and legal confirmation of the relationship. It was the custom almost invariably observed, however, that the bride continued to live at home with her parents for about a year, and she would not normally have been alone with the man during that time (though some exceptions are mentioned). But she is definitely married, and any breach of the contract by man or wife would be legally adultery. After a year, the bride moves in with her husband — the point which has evidently been reached by Joseph and Mary. The angel therefore says to him, 'Do not be afraid to take your wife Mary to your home,' which is the formal 'transferral' that follows a Jewish marriage.

Melchizedek to Noah's brother's wife, Sopanim. The story-line comes so close to virgin birth that many scholars had previously assumed it must reflect the Gospel version, and so be a Christian late insertion in the Jewish text of *2 Enoch.* Yet Sopanim simply is not a virgin, but an abstinent. The real miracles are her conception in old age, parallel to Elizabeth rather than Mary, and the even greater miracle of life from death.

The virgin-birth theme is a sign of the Saoshyant idea which brought together and arranged in a prophetological cycle the heroic sagas and stories. It has definitely influenced the *Apocalypse of Adam,* and the virgin-birth aspect is explicit in a number of the stories in its twelvefold sequence of the manifestations of the Illuminator, the ever-appearing prophet of Light. Moreover, several of the virgin-birth themes occur in a single block of material that closely parallels the infancy stories in Matthew. But unfortunately once more (for Brown's hypothesis, that is), this does not bring the virgin birth theme any closer to Luke, for the simple reason that while Luke reproduces some of the disturbing-nativity themes, he has no echoes at all of the other segments (oppression, escape and exile; the visit from pagan prophet-priests). The resemblances Brown finds in Luke relate only to the equivalent of the Zal-segment, as we now know it to be — and this does not have a virgin birth.

So the virgin birth cannot have come to Luke from a common tradition shared with Matthew. Luke shares narrative traditions only with parts of Matthew that do not reflect a pre-existing virgin-birth story.

The great scholar's theory collapses. It looked so plausible when it was associated with purely analytical and hypothetical sources. But the recovery of the actual stories, both separately in some cases, and already joined in a cycle in the *Apocalypse of Adam,* punctures it fatally by showing that the details derive from very specific legends. At the very moment it strikingly affirms the fundamental rightness of the threefold analysis of Matthew 1–2, it removes one crucial detail that would have enabled us to link Luke also with one of the narrative lines.

So where did Luke get his concept of the virgin birth? The best option seems to be that he got it, not from sources shared with Matthew — but from Matthew's Gospel itself. For in a far more general way, New Testament scholarship has been trying for the last century and more to prove that Matthew and Luke share common sources, and they have persuaded the theological establishment that it must be true, perhaps by the sheer insistence that it must be so. Yet they have not been able to prove it. (If one wanted to be critical, one might intimate to these scholars that it is hardly possible to prove something when there are no confirmatory materials outside those needing to be explained: there is something logically askew here.) By the nature of the case, what has to be proved is that Matthew and Luke evince signs of shared materials or sources that are not found, e.g. in the Gospel of Mark. We need something that is in Matthew and Luke but not anywhere else, so any 'third factor' is ruled out. Matthew and Luke do have some of the same material, some of which is not in Mark. But that does not really logically entitle you to say that the shared material necessarily comes from a common extra source — the so called 'Q'-document, from German *Quelle,* source.

These are the perils of developing a theory which is not based on external evidence. There is hardly any other remaining discipline outside the theological faculties where one is allowed simply to make up the evidence when you need it. And on philosophical grounds it is logically objectionable in this instance, because there is a straightforward explanation that does not involve an unconfirmed hypothetical documentary source. The simple explanation is that Luke contains material not in Mark, but also found in Matthew, because he has been able to draw on the latter Gospel. Luke is after all the most literary of the Gospels, already referring at the outset of his work to other written accounts. He is quite certainly writing a little later than Mark or Matthew, and he is just as certainly aware of the writings that were achieving prominence in the Church. Matthew's Gospel was, even after Luke's time, much more influential than any of the others.

The new theory, or 'paradigm' of the relationship between Gospels has been worked out in great technical detail by Michael Goulder, and is convincing increasing numbers of the experts. From what was said previously, e.g. about the genealogies, it will be obvious that Luke, on the other hand, should not be therefore be thought of as a mere imitator of Matthew. He writes a Gospel of his own because he sees the story from a different angle, and has his own emphases — often quite different from Matthew's. For instance, he stresses the priestly aspect, rather than the royal legends of Matthew. If he presents an analogy, but also a different story from Matthew, it makes it all the more clear that he is indicating something different: so much so that in the genealogy, we may recall, it seemed as though he were almost suggesting another figure altogether, whose priestly ancestry may have had a special meaning for Luke.

Interestingly, one of the pioneers of the approach, now recognized as essential, which treats each Gospel not just as a collection of traditions but as an interpretation and literary realization of them with a distinctive character and aim, was Rudolf Steiner. No-one commented more illuminatingly on the differences between the Gospels as a way of understanding their deeper meaning. Yet when he comes to discuss the virginal conception of Jesus in his lectures on *The Gospel of Matthew,* he speaks in a striking way about both Matthew and Luke. In Matthew he finds a reference to the Holy Spirit as the creative, cosmic power of God, working in the generations of humanity from Abraham down to the immediate ancestors of Jesus — something very similar, in other words, to the historical and prophetic working of the Spirit in the *Gospel of the Hebrews.* There is nothing to suggest divine paternity — the 'superficial understanding,' as he puts it, of the 'exoteric interpretations of the virgin birth.' And then he adds a further comment:

> Such is the sacred meaning, infinitely greater than any superficial interpretation, of the 'conception by the Holy Spirit of the cosmos' [= Matt.1:18]. It is also the basis of the

saying that she who gave birth to this one was to be 'filled
with the power of the Spirit of the cosmos' [= Luke 1:35].*

Steiner was certainly not trying here to work out the literary
relations of the Gospels. But he was indicating the derivation of
a central idea. The meaning of Matthew's phrase referring to her
'being with child — by the Holy Spirit,' then, he regards as also
the basis of Luke's passage where the angel promises that upon
her will come the Spirit and power of God. This is quite remarkable. Though he considered that Luke was trying to build up an
understanding of Jesus from quite a different angle to Matthew,
he derives the Lukan idea from the concept which is to be found
in Matthew's infancy narrative concerning the virgin birth. Even
if, as we must admit, it would be misleading to regard this as evidence for a literary connection, it does unmistakably affirm the
original identity of the Lukan idea with that in Matthew.

Luke, however, was to bring out its implications quite differently, and in relation to his own distinctive 'priestly' figure of
Jesus. To see how he does so, we need to look more generally at
the way he presents the story of Jesus' birth, and try to fathom
the distinctive approach which underlies it. This is to go straight
to the heart of the whole Gospel of Luke. For his Gospel is in a
quite unique way, as we may still appreciate and admire today,
the Christmas Gospel.

The Christmas Gospel proclaimed

It has become a commonplace for Bible-scholars and commen-
tators to stress Luke's sense of history, and also for that very
reason his special openness to historical influences, connections
and perspectives. From the beginning of the Gospel he speaks of

* Rudolf Steiner, (1985) *The Gospel of St. Matthew,* London and New York,
p.80. Steiner rightly takes the Semitic idiom in the Lukan phrase, 'Spirit and
the power' as 'power of the Spirit.'

world-events connected with the Roman Empire, and in doing so he is implicitly both comparing and contrasting Christ with the *divus Augustus,* the God-emperor whose power had established peace throughout the known world. It was in many ways the Roman Empire which had stimulated awareness of history in the sense we now know it (building on but transforming an older notion from the Greeks). After all, the rise of the Roman power had changed the lives of millions of people and brought them in touch with one another, so that the question of how it all came about and how to respond had an urgency beyond any academic discipline. The Roman conception then came together rather powerfully with the Jewish and Old Testament idea of God's working in history. Already in the Book of Daniel, the great world-empires before Rome had been seen as under divine sway and judgment.

We must remember too that the Roman *imperium* was not just a worldly power, but was associated everywhere with the cult of the Emperor, and the worship of the goddess Roma; even the standards or banners of the legions were sacral objects, the loss of which to the enemy was an act of sacrilege as well as humiliating defeat. The Hellenistic world and the Middle East had known 'divine rulers' in the past. The Emperors inherited their mantle, but never before had the concept been joined with such personal and absolute authority. History has reached a special moment, and the 'peace of Augustus' seemed to mark the climax of the destiny of Rome. Yet Christ's birth is something greater than this for Luke and his Gospel. Christianity will not be a world-empire (though sadly that distinction was later not always kept in mind), but a universal advent of God's saving love and mercy.

The Roman Empire had also in practice brought religious tolerance and the acceptance of many different cults and faiths. These were protected by legal safeguards, though this meant that unacknowledged religions could be persecuted as being mere 'superstition,' a fate from which early Christianity was not always exempt. Luke's stress on the biblical and Jewish-Temple background of Christianity (e.g. in the intertwined story of

Zechariah and the birth of the Baptist) thus has an oddly Gentile meaning as well as a Jewish one, reflecting the situation of Lukan Christianity: it helps establish that Christianity is the 'true Judaism,' and so a genuine religion worthy of imperial status. At any rate it is within a vision of world-wide spiritual history that Luke's presentation of Christianity belongs, taking as its starting-point the Augustan *pax universalis* but indicating the true meaning of God's kingdom upon earth. The fact that there are echoes of other religions in the early chapters especially does not derive from the Roman Empire, of course. But the understanding of the world-aspirations of Judaism in its Christian form does rely on the consciousness of the imperial world-order among those to whom it was addressed.

There are, for example, themes that appear to point to oriental religion. They feature especially and in particularly beautiful form in the early chapters, so that it is tempting to think that the great revelations of the past seem to appear one last time to humanity in angelic splendour and in allusive pictures and inspirations, before being subsumed up and taken forward into the Christian story. The message of love and compassion had been heard before, in the East, in the teaching of Buddha. Recently a scholar studying the infancy narratives suggested that Indian themes and stories must have come to Luke's attention, possibly through the Gnostics who were fascinated by cults of inner knowledge and illumination and might well have been interested in Buddhism. Luke was certainly in places trying to reinterpret what seemed to be one-sided emphases in Gnostic Christianity, and is himself almost obsessed with visions, dreams and revelations. Eastern ideas thus mingle with more familiar background. The message of hope had been heard before, in the Old Testament prophets. And in the world-historical setting of Luke's vision, a greater vision still must now absorb all these spiritual themes into the new faith of Christianity.

Take the story of Shimeon. The old man has been waiting in the Temple many years, patiently expecting the 'consolation of Israel,' that is to say, the fulfilment of its Messianic hopes, after all the sufferings of the Jewish people. One may note that the scene strikingly resembles one in Buddhist tradition. In Buddhism, the sage Asita was the old man who had recognized the child Gautama as the future Buddha, or Enlightened One, who would achieve liberation and bring release to the world. His joyful recognition is touched, however by a note of sorrow and even existential pain — for he himself was destined not to live long enough to see it. He will need to be reincarnated again and again, striving through many lives for Enlightenment, before he can encounter the teaching of such a one as the Buddha.

Now Christianity in Luke's Gospel brings a similar vision, and yet is able to add something just as significant to it. It is as though the former Asita's destiny is lived out once again in the patiently hopeful Shimeon. He experiences again the 'Buddhistic' moment of recognizing a child who will bring salvation. But the burden of *karma,* the almost interminably long effort to reach Enlightenment that would need many further lives, which dominates the Buddhist story, is transformed in Simeon's experience into a Christian hope. Shimeon senses something which has no place in the Buddhist world-view. He feels that history is nearing its climax, when the promised redeemer will come for all people. He feels that events are moving in accordance with the plan of the Sovereign Lord to whom he gives thanks. And so his own sense of loss is swallowed up in a greater thankfulness. Historical consciousness brings a sense of shared fulfilment that enables him to 'depart in peace,' knowing that humanity will reach its goal. The scene grows out of Buddhism, and in recapitulating it Luke in no way need deny its roots there; but it gains another dimension: a Christian and 'historical' reality which is central to Luke's universalism and appreciation of God's loving, merciful guidance of events.

Shimeon's sense of the drama of redemption as something that has begun to unroll, to be realized in history, so that he can die consoled, is also our sense as we read the early chapters of the Gospel. Even though the 'consolation' has not outwardly actually happened yet, Shimeon can feel satisfied in the knowledge that it will indeed come. And it is in that same sense that the virgin-born child lying in the manger, whom the angels call a 'sign,' is already from the outset the Messiah-as-Lord (*Christos Kyrios,* a strange, concentinated sort of phrase in the original Greek) — already the Saviour who will be hailed as *Kyrios* (the risen Lord) in the Church after his death. Matthew tells a nativity story which brings us face to face, so to speak, with the Man, the one whom we must decide to acknowledge — or not — as the Messiah, the fulfiller of the biblical prophecies. 'Doesn't this prophecy or that prove it?' he seems to ask us: 'Do you not recognize that he was the One?' And his story comes to an end, in that sense, if he has been able to make the reader recognize that at every point Jesus was acting as the one who was destined to make God's presence manifest among us. The Spirit finds in him its eschatological 'Rest.' Mark's opening baptism-scene shows Jesus acknowledged by divine acclamation, the Son of God; to his cosmic authority the daemonic beings bow. John's peerless prologue leads us up into spiritual worlds. Both Mark and John stress the breaking in of a timeless truth. But Luke gives us the special sense that we are called on to be part of a wonderful unfolding sequence of events, which even in their beginning are a 'sign' that the process of spiritual transformation has begun, whose goal is humanity's salvation. That is why I said that it is in a very specific sense the Christmas Gospel, since the central message of Christianity is for Luke already contained, implicitly, in the sign of the crib at Bethlehem. When we see it, with spiritual acceptance, we realize from that moment on that we are taking part in the saving history which will transform us, along with all of humanity that is willing to join us, and lead us to God.

Highly significant to Luke's Gospel therefore is the repeated recurrence to the angelic message:

> Glory in the spiritual heights,
> Peace on earth to men of good will.

— even at the very end where one might expect that it would at last have been displaced in our minds by the emblem of the Cross on Golgotha. For the Gospel never does really go beyond that Christmas revelation, nor does it need to, but only to unfold it from changing angles as spiritual-historical events unroll. For example, Raymond Brown has noted that it is Luke alone who gives us later, in chapter 19, when Jesus makes his triumphal entry as the Messiah, something once more strangely similar to the angelic song. A multitude of disciples cries out:

> Peace in heaven,
> and glory in the spiritual heights.

'It is a fascinating touch,' he observes, 'that the multitude of the heavenly host proclaims peace on earth, while a multitude of earthly disciples proclaims peace in heaven.' As a matter of fact, the counterpointing continues, for example right into the resurrection appearances of chapter 24, where Jesus now appears among the disciples on earth and proclaims 'Peace among you,' promising that they themselves will soon be 'clothed with power from the spiritual heights.'

Luke thinks here in accord with the Greek conception of history, which tends to look for something whole and explicable that determines the events from beginning to end. Some of the Stoic philosophers even thought that since everything follows a definite law, what had happened once would necessarily be played out again and again, and all of us would live and die just as we are in future cycles of time. To live in accord with such a law of events, consciously acquiescing in it, was the Stoic ideal of the wise man. Luke, though he does not follow the excesses of Stoic literalism, also implies that events on earth from the nativity onward are harmonized with a heavenly law, uniting earthly and cosmic reality. He invites us to recognize and live in accordance with this revealed reality of the divine, showing itself through 'signs' here below. We will then be part of the unfolding events of salvation-history. In a view of this kind, history does not essentially produce anything new. The same essence behind events shows itself from the beginning, from the first 'sign' of the Messiah-Kyrios as a baby still lying in the feed-trough to the realization of the bewildered disciples of Jesus' divine nature on the road to Emmaus and after.

The result of this conception of history is that Luke can see already in the baby Jesus, in a way not possible for Matthew, the dying-and-risen Lord, the Son of God. As the angel of annunciation says:

> The Holy Spirit will come upon you, and the Power from
> the Most High will overshadow you. Therefore the child to
> be born will be called holy — the Son of God.

Matthew's stories point to Jesus as the one who will be the promised climax of the cycle, the bearer of the destiny brought to him by the Spirit of God. But Luke can regard the same event as a divine birth, already containing in its essence the whole of the reality of salvation. To understand what he has to say about it, we need to draw upon a very different background of ideas.

6. The Son of God

The ox and the ass

Where did Luke go to find ideas that could express his concept of Jesus' divine birth? Certainly not to the Old Testament prophecies of the Messiah, who is God's agent of renewal and ruler of his People in the last times, but not a supernatural or divine being. Nor was it even to the more esoteric Judaism that underlies Matthew's age-long preparation of the Prophet through the cycles of time and generations. This was a providence of the Holy Spirit, already active in bringing about the birth of Jesus, but a working which reaches its goal, or 'finds Rest,' at the baptism in the Jordan, when Jesus in the Hebrew Gospel was hailed by the divine voice as 'my beloved Son, whose reign is for ever.' But for the idea that the birth of Jesus itself was a revelation from the heights of divine mercy and love, transfiguring the peace of earth, Luke had to look to other backgrounds of ideas. And curiously, the clue to his search is to be found in the humblest, least likely component in the story: the presence of the ox and the ass.

The Egyptians had long been fascinated by the life of nature, and in particular by the many animals which abound there, and which seemed to them to embody different aspects of the gods. Anyone who has been to Egypt and experienced the stark contrast between the surrounding desert landscape and the long ribbon of the Nile and its incredibly fertile plain will immediately understand why. There can be no question here of setting up a civilization of humans only, to which the animals and 'wild' nature are 'outside' and alien to man's life. The River, together with the unfailing Sun, is the source of all life for human beings and animals, who must share it and be constantly reminded of their common setting and the way it makes possible every detail and pattern of their lives. The gods themselves are the eternal and indestructible life in the sun-drenched landscape of Egypt, the Land, the River and all that manifests its vitality. By being at one with that universal life, that is, by taking part in the rites and cultus of the gods of Egypt, human beings too could actually share in the spiritual dimension of nature's being. One of them, the Pharaoh, was so identified with the life-giving and ordering power that was immanent in the very landscape, the River, the Sun that rose every day, that he was a god on earth — the living Horus.

Far from conceiving nature as a stubborn environment whose 'Dark' intransigence had to be subdued, cultivated and opened to the Light and so made to yield its abundance with the help of human beings, as did the archaic Iranians, the Egyptians could only experience their reliance on the divinely ordained cycles of the flooding of the Nile, the circuit of the Sun and beyond that the stars. All seemed eternal and unalterable. They were completely a part of it. The Egyptians themselves worked creatively like forces of nature, not only in co-operating with the Nile-flood to grow their food but in their architecture and art: a cliff could be carved into monumental figures, a tomb could be shaped as a great mountain towering up to heaven. And human time too seemed to flow on in cycles, ever repeating themselves. The Egyptians had little sense of the changeable in history, unlike the little vulnerable kingdom of the Jews, so often a pawn between the great superpowers of the antique world (Assyrians, Babylonians, Egyptians, Persians). One Pharaonic victory over foreigners in the borderlands only seemed to the Egyptians only to repeat the preserving deed of all previous Pharaohs to maintain inviolate order of the Land. Depictions of his victory show type-cast foreign enemies subdued, with typical names — the same figures, and even the same names repeated on similar monuments centuries apart! Life ever renewed itself and was ever the same divinely ordered life. After death, it seemed beyond doubt that the soul that could attach itself to the destiny of the ever-reborn Sun-god, Re, and caught up in its diurnal journey would travel to the timeless twinkling heaven of the stars. For the same renewing life that is in everything is also in us. The cycles, like life, are eternal and holy.

Birth was not conceived by ancient Egyptian thought, therefore, as an absolute beginning. It too was part of a cycle, and was not essentially different from the other cycles of which the Egyptians felt themselves a part. The Sun travelled every night through the dark belly of the sky-cow, Nut, studded with stars, and could be thought of as 'born' every morning — or conversely, birth could be thought of as analogous to the daily (or yearly) rising of the Sun. Such analogies focussed naturally upon the Pharaoh, who was ever the link between humanity and the divine. He was divinely born, and his birth was a cosmic birth like that of the sun, though of course it was a human birth too, though specially touched by the divine. And in late Egyptian times the divine was conceived in particular as 'Spirit,' personified in Amun. His easily recognizable feather-symbol among the hieroglyphs shows the underlying conception to be that of an invisible moving power, like the wind or breath. But all the gods existed in a similar, spiritual way, so that Re the Sun-god became one manifestation of the Spirit: Amun-Re. It is therefore in the theology of the Pharaoh's divine birth, and some of the legends associated with it, that we find the most plausible background to the idea of a man's divine birth as actually effected by the divine Spirit. The child was 'breathed in' to the mortal mother: the phrase is still used in the Hermetic Mysteries contemporary with Christian beginnings where it is applied to the divine being begotten within us, the Son of God, generated through the mystical 'in-breathing,' according to the tract *On Rebirth* (Corpus Hermeticum XIII). The Hermetists are undoubtedly echoing an older Egyptian idea. Pharaoh came into being from a god's breath of life, and was reputed to have the power of life or death as a result.

When the Sun is born in the morning, in ancient Egyptian texts, he is hailed and praised by the whole world of creatures, and the Egyptians were aware that human beings are not alone, or even foremost, in giving thanks for the reappearance of light after the darkness of night. Before human eyes have even seen the Sun, when he is still under the eastern horizon, the animals are stirring to life, and their gestures and sounds were experienced as a celebration of the life the Sun brings. In another picture, the Sun could be described as climbing the eastern mountain: we must remember that the Egyptians thought much more pictorially, and that the pictures are ideas, ways of thinking which complement each other; we must not take them too heavily, as if they were supposed to be nineteenth-century scientific theories redolent of a Gradgrind. At any rate, on the eastern Mountain the Sun was worshipped by the baboons and other creatures, chattering their hymns. And by an extension of the picture very typical of mythological thinking, even before the Sun was hailed by the creatures just on this side of the margins of our known world, it must already have been hailed by those creatures on the other side of the margin, the fabulous and exotic animals of the 'horizon dwellers' who saw the Sun while it was still invisible to us.

Like the Sun, a Pharaoh when he is born comes as the life-bearing presence of the divine to the world-order he inherits, restoring peace and harmony after the dangerous time of the interregnum. It was inevitable that the world which welcomed him should be not only the human one, but that of the animals too, with which human life along the Nile-ribbon was so inseparably linked. The presence of the ox and the ass in the Lukan story of Jesus' birth has convinced many scholars of the Gospels nowadays that 'the roots of the concept of the birth of the divine child, who will usher in the new age, lie in Egyptian mythology and mystery language ... The theme of peace among the animals ... has a firm place in ancient Egyptian enthronement language' (Helmut Koester). Moreover, we know that this language and the religious feeling that it inspired was quite widespread at the time of Christian origins, for it appears also in the wonderful 'Fourth Eclogue' of the Roman poet Vergil. He is, so to speak, the official prophet of Augustus' new age of peace. He prophesies the birth of a child and the return of the Age of Gold, when all nature and the animals will be in harmony. And strikingly, it all begins with the return of a heavenly 'virgin' — Justice who according to mythology had fled in horror from the fallen world of human beings and taken refuge above. But now, with an astrological cross-reference also clearly in mind — now that Virgin returns (*Iam redit et Virgo ...*). Once more, therefore, the rising of a star and a heavenly Virgin lead in the new time, and a child is born.

The early Christians were all convinced that Vergil was speaking here of the fulfilment of the biblical prophecies of the Messiah — and in fact they may have been right. Certainly Vergil may have known Jewish sources, perhaps indirectly through the Jewish Sibylline prophecies. Some of the Jewish prophets, moreover, were already profoundly influenced by the Mystery-ideas from Egypt. Although Isaiah's supposed reference to the virgin birth was something of a red-herring, we are on firmer ground in noting that in another less obscure passage about a child being born, Isaiah 9:6 uses familiar royal and even divine language:

> He shall be called Wonderful Counsellor, Mighty God,
> Everlasting Father, the Prince of Peace ...

Exactly such titles were used of the Pharaoh at his accession. And Isaiah's famous passage on the lion lying down with the lamb also seems to reflect the well-known royal myth. Moses Hadas has argued that Vergil could have known these passages from the Jewish Bible more or less directly; but the point is not altogether important, for in a deeper sense, his imagination was certainly drawing on the same 'Mystery-language' and imagination that features in them and in the background of the Lukan nativity.

Once again, therefore, we must be aware that Luke is deliberately counterposing his version of universal salvation against that of the Roman imperial propaganda. The true inheritor of the vision that had come down from the Mysteries, concerning divine birth and a new era of the world, he is saying, was not mighty Augustus Caesar but the baby Jesus who was, for those who could discern the 'sign,' the destined Messiah-Kyrios, the triumphant

Son of God. He was describing a picture that would have been familiar to many of his readers in the Hellenistic-Roman world, which was accustomed to the idea that a true world-ruler was specially favoured and even specially begotten through divine agency — though exactly how was a secret of the Mysteries, like those of the Hermetists, revealed only to those who were worthy of higher knowledge. His path thus runs parallel to the one which we have seen generated the images and ideas behind Matthew's stories, which all came from esoteric movements and ideas in the Jewish world.

Some of the older researchers, in the headier days when 'comparative religion' was blowing away the cobwebs of dogmatic theology and placing Christianity for the first time into the stream of world-religions in their historical development, simply concluded that the whole story of the virgin birth came into Christianity from Egyptian mythology. But that does not seem very likely. For one thing, it looks as though Luke was rather responding to Matthew's account of the virgin birth. What he took from current religious ideas was the means, therefore, of presenting what, on one level, one might see simply as a translation into terms and images that were equivalent for the slightly different, gentile and Hellenistic audience he was writing for.

He was also bringing out more of the 'priestly' significance of Jesus, from his special point of view. The Pharaoh too, of course, was the highest priest as well as ruler in the Egyptian world, and he alone was able to perform the holiest rites. And Egypt itself, with its recurring cycles of climate and inundation, was conceived as in its totality a mighty temple in which all life was an ever re-enacted rite.

But the problem is that the divine begetting of the Pharaoh was not originally a virgin birth, though it was a supernatural one. We may surmise therefore that the story in Luke's Gospel has behind it a process of subtle evolution, and cannot be seen as simply taken over artificially from Egyptian myth and applied to Jesus. Possibly the way was again prepared in some of those mysterious Jewish-esoteric sects we have constantly referred to. The

Essenes, for instance, had already elevated the Priestly Messiah over the traditional Davidic, royal Messiah. And the role of the virgin in a divine birth also appears for the first time in Jewish sources. We need to investigate more closely.

A divine child

First of all let us look at the pagan sources who tell us about the Egyptian theology of the divine child.

The most relevant of these is the Greek author Plutarch, best known for his series of *Parallel Lives,* but also important as a religious thinker and one of the few sources we have who speaks of the ancient Mysteries at first hand. He is writing in the early Christian period. It is in his 'Life of Numa' (ch.4) that he speaks of the Egyptian mystical ideas of birth:

> The Egyptians are of the opinion that a supernatural in-
> tercourse with a mortal woman on the part of a god is not
> beyond the bounds of possibility. The Spirit draws near to her,
> they say, and begets in her the germinal beginnings of life.

It was, however, only a woman who could receive a divine impregnation, and the theory did not hold with the idea of a mortal man begetting offspring on a female deity. The nature of a god was seminal as being composed of air and spirit, and could come together with the warmth and watery nature in the womb. (In this opinion the Egyptians were entirely in accord with Greek mythology, which knows of many divinely begotten heroes; but it recounts only cautionary tales of those mortal men who like Tantalus or Ixion had designs upon a goddess.) Very similar conceptions are reported also by Philo of Alexandria, the mystical and allegorical Jewish philosopher, at much the same period.

Their origin, concludes Eduard Norden in his fascinating and far-seeking study on *The Birth of the Child,* undoubtedly does lie in the royal and priestly lore of ancient Egypt. 'There the belief in the descent of the ruling monarch from the Sun-god Amun-Re had been held since time immemorial, and changes of dynasty over the millennia had left it unchanged.' The priestly theology explained that on the occasion of their first intercourse, the god took on the guise of the King and united with the Queen, i.e. before she has any human sexual contact. The Queen's first child is thus divinely begotten; it is this which explains the qualities of the Pharaoh. Note here the rather precise correspondence to the situation of Mary, who has 'not yet had contact with a man' though she has a mortal husband, but bears a first-born child through the Spirit, who will be called Son of God. Indeed, the insistence of Luke on mentioning that Jesus is her 'first-born' has otherwise perplexed the interpreters (2:7).

The prototype of the divine birth in ancient Egypt is, however, a further and a deeper Mystery. For the hereditary transmission of the kingship is a reflection of the profound cyclicity of the Egyptian world-view, whose ultimate expression is found in the symbolism of the dying god Osiris. If the birth of the Pharaoh is attended by the imaginative suggestion of god's Spirit becoming man, the death of the Pharaoh is transfigured by the suggestion of man becoming a god. On a further level of myth and inner meaning, the birth of the living god and the death of his previous earthly vehicle are strangely related.

Death and birth

Gods are not supposed to die. We cannot exaggerate the paradox involved in the fact that Osiris, one of the important early gods in the divine family of Heliopolis (the City of the Sun), died. It was unheard of.

We can hear something of what it meant from an ancient Egyptian account of the trial of the evil god Seth for murdering him and seizing his kingdom, a case brought by Osiris' son Horus. The trial was held before the divine Ennead, the Nine Great Gods, and presided over by the Lord of the Universe in person, and has been beautifully brought to life in a recent book by Dimitri Meeks. The issues were of course remarkably clear cut, since the crime in question is an emblematic one, representing the very struggle of evil against good. Despite Seth's outrageous protestations that *he* is the injured party, and his proposal to solve the question by fighting Horus, the gods realize that by any sort of justice Horus is in the right in claiming back his patrimony. Thoth, who is Wisdom itself, agrees. The case seems about to end. But they have reckoned without the disgruntled Lord of the Universe. To their astonishment, he favours the diabolical Seth over his own son Osiris, and is about to give him everything he has so criminally obtained; evidently he is impressed by his ruthlessness, and thinks he will be a useful ally in running the universe.

The gods are appalled, and Thoth objects to this unconstitutional approach. Reluctantly, the Supreme has to accept arbitration by some outside party. Unfortunately, few gods are prepared to step into the hot issue and give a decisive judgment. The case drags on for eighty years. As a last ditch attempt, the tribunal turns to the great and mysterious goddess of Sais, Neith. The Creator himself has to be respectful of her, and in the extremely polite letter which he writes setting out the case we at last get a sense of what has made him so disgusted with Osiris and dismissive of his grandson's claims:

> The creator began with a plaint. While Sobek [the crocodile god], he said, Neith's son, gave his mother no cause for concern, he, the king of the gods, had a son who had conceived the unhappy idea of getting himself killed, a circumstance that was causing him no end of trouble as far as the royal succession was concerned. He had decided to put the matter into the goddess's hands.

Neith responds with impeccable moral clarity, totally for Horus, absolutely condemning Seth. Even then, the Creator goes into a fury, suspends the court without appointing a day for resuming the trial, and storms off. Eventually Horus has to reclaim his inheritance by overcoming Seth in single combat; the defeated god of evil is banished from Egypt into the desert, though he still troubles the gods from time to time. Crucial to the tale, however, is the fact that Osiris has done what no god ought to do — how could he even think about doing something like dying? Though he was morally wronged, it is hard even for the Supreme Creator, his father, to take his side.

The Egyptians felt that death was an anomaly in the world order, just as strongly as we moderns may feel that evil is an anomaly. How can God be good if innocent children suffer in their millions from disease, poverty or starvation? This troubles us deeply, existentially, but the Egyptians felt still more deeply that the world could make no sense at all if the anomaly of death was found in it. It contradicted everything we said about the Egyptian sense of its eternal order and permanence. Osiris, however, is the god who gave a deeper meaning to death. And the context is the royal succession — as ever the link between the world of mortals and the gods. Without the royal succession, therefore, the human world, Egypt, would lose contact with the divine realm, and the world itself would then grow old and die. (There is a powerful description of just that in the Hermetic tractate *Asclepius*.) Though he is externally a powerful king, the priestly role of the Pharaoh as the one who joins humanity to the eternal world of the gods is even more important. Indeed, his whole existence is a sort of sacramental one.

Osiris is the meaning of death, and when the Pharaoh dies he overcomes the anomalous, meaningless nature of death precisely because he 'becomes Osiris.' Later, others could likewise share in his destiny and become Osiris after their death. At the foundation of the myth lies an archaic form of initiation — death and rebirth on a higher, divine plane, which ensured that after death the initiated person did not perish utterly but his higher part returned to the eternal realm of the stars. Subsequently the practices of initiation took that special Egyptian form of elaborate mortuary ritual. Through their enactment, people much more widely could ensure a higher spiritual place for themselves in the afterlife. But the Pharaoh is the supreme model and original of the whole process. As the reigning king he is the living Horus, the Sun-god in human form shining upon his people; as the deceased monarch he is Osiris, the god who died.

But that is only to pose the problem of the succession: how can the successor become the true living god? The rupture of death defeated the very order of creation at the trial, as represented by the Creator's inability to cope with the fact that Osiris had involved himself with, of all things, death. In other words, the problem of true, divine succession cannot be solved on any outward level, through constitutional process, etc. etc. Such things are necessary to running the world, but they do not give the answer to its inner meaning.

The new Pharaoh can only be known to be the true living Horus on the basis of a spiritual, not an outward connection to his predecessor. There must be the outer descent, but also something more: an inner, mystical birth. And the story of it was told as follows. When Osiris was murdered, the demonic Seth scattered his limbs and hid them in many different places, so as to prevent him from continuing his existence in any way. His identity was thoroughly dissipated. The devoted Isis his wife, however, sought through the world to find them and carefully reassembled them, like the mummifiers carefully preserving the limbs of the deceased and arranging them as in life. Though he was dead, Osiris thus regained a sort of purely spiritual integrity, a shadow of existence; he was once again a force in the world. And though he was purely imaginal, virtual so to speak, he created in Isis the germinal seed of life, which became his son Horus. The living Pharaoh gains his true authority and divine existence at the moment his predecessor dies, and mystically begets him from beyond the grave, as Osiris begetting Horus. Or one could say that the divine life in the Pharaoh lives on from generation to generation, mystically reborn in the next king whenever one dies. Thus even his death becomes a significant part of the cosmic order, being yet one more source of continuing life.

This birth is something much higher than the event touched on earlier, where the Queen-mother is touched by a power of the Spirit when she conceives the first child. It is in a much higher sense a divine birth, and brings in the new age, the new reign of a god on earth.

But in neither instance is there truly a virgin birth, since the myth is actually that of a male god begetting a son on a woman or a goddess. In both cases there is conception without a normal human act of fertilization, creating a paradox which solves the logically insoluble problem of the succession of life. But the theory in both instances presents a fairly elaborate case for the seminal potency of the Spirit when joined with a warm and watery nature, or for the integrity of the spiritual form that exists even when the outer form is dead, and is able to effect the conception of a son. The ideas could certainly fascinate and influence any who took the trouble to ponder and divine their implications, however; and in Christianity the notion of a death that becomes the source of rebirth into eternal life was certainly present, though rather different in form. The life-and-death mysticism of the Succession Myth might well have been part of what attracted the Egyptian stories of divine birth into the sphere of the Gospel narrative, along with the idea of a new era commencing. But it probably also acquired a colouring on the way from Judaism, which had of course long had a powerful presence in Alexandria, and other parts of Egypt as well.

As a well-educated Alexandrian intellectual, Philo Judaeus would naturally have been aware of the patterns of thought which belonged to Egyptian life, especially since, as we have seen, they had become quite widely known, at least in their externals, in the Graeco-Roman world (Plutarch, etc.). His entire life's work comprised a commentary on the books of the Bible which showed that they contained all the wisdom of philosophy and Greek scientific thought in an allegorical manner. The greater part of this monumental enterprise has actually survived. Though it proved useless to Judaism in the very different circumstances which prevailed after the suppression of the Temple and destruction of Jerusalem

(AD 70), his commentaries were extremely useful to Christians, who had to present the biblical message increasingly in a gentile environment. Luke himself stands at the beginning of this phase, and although we cannot say that he knew Philo's work as such, he was certainly aware of the trends which are written large within it. Philo was not unique — just more thorough and erudite, no doubt, than most of his like-minded contemporaries. Many other minds were struggling to bridge the Jewish-Hellenistic divide.

Philo discusses the Egyptian mystic ideas of birth in a passage of his *On the Cherubim* (chs.12–15) and in a number of places elsewhere. He describes the idea as a great and holy mystery that has been handed down, and he considers that it is based upon the truth that is described in the Bible in the narratives about the Patriarchs. The passage is rather long and rambling, but its essential point is clear. As in the case of Sarah, Abraham's wife, for example, who had borne him no children: when he will, God descends upon the womb of such pure-minded, virginal mortal women in order to engender in them a child. The description of the drawing near and engendering process given by Philo is so similar to that in Plutarch's 'Egyptian' theology of the Spirit that it can hardly be doubted that it comes from the same source. What we notice immediately, of course, is that Philo has heavily qualified the old pagan ideas of a sexual or quasi-sexual potency of the divine Spirit, and insisted upon the virginal state of the mortal woman favoured in this way by God. In the instance of the elderly Sarah it is quite hard to make literal sense of her 'virginity' — but such concerns were never very strong with the adept in finding an allegory at every turn. The important point is that Philo has adopted into Judaism, albeit in the guise of allegory, a version of divine generation which he has purified of any suggested impropriety by insisting upon its strictly virginal nature. God does not 'beget' a son in a male role as father, but supernaturally causes her to give birth.

For Philo, all this relates to the inner life of the soul. He interprets 'Sarah' as 'my sovereignty,' and takes her as the soul's power of self-control, i.e. wisdom, which has sovereignty over every virtuous soul. Hence he describes his own education in terms of an approach to Sarah, so that she should become fruitful for him: her offspring being, of course, the virtues ('good words, blameless thoughts and praiseworthy actions'). At first, however, she remains barren for him:

> For in my youthfulness I was not yet able to receive her offspring, wisdom, justice, piety, because of the multitude of bastard children whom empty imaginings had borne in me ... It is well then to pray that virtue may not only engender (she is prolific even without our prayers), but also that she may engender for ourselves, so that we may share in what she sows and produces and be truly happy. For she customarily engenders for God alone, thankfully rendering the first-fruits of the goods she has obtained to him who, as Moses says, opens the ever-virgin womb.

He is at pains to stress yet again that:

> We must exclude from the present discussion bodily unions or intercourse having pleasure as its object. The union in question is a mating of mind with virtue, a mind desirous of having children by her.

Thus Philo in his *On the Intercourse which is for the Sake of Learning.*

It is always hard to tell how far abstract ideas and allegories have any reality beyond their immediate context. Certainly it would be a bizarre thought that Joseph was really an empty-headed student going through his preliminary education and had not yet attained the heights of mature intellect, so that Mary was able to bring forth her child wisdom to God alone, in a virginal conception to him who 'opens the ever-virgin womb.' More realistically, such allegories are able to sustain any meaning only because the underlying concepts have an existence independently in the culture to which the writer belongs, and the flimsy logical connections are sustained by patterns of thinking that actually draw their coherence from elsewhere. Some scholars have even thought that there must have been a Jewish Mystery-cult to which Philo belonged, in which these ideas would gel in the minds of those who held them, a closed group. That theory however has many historical problems to face. It is much more likely that such patterns of thought were derived from widespread cultural assumptions, tortuously given a special biblical reference by such ingenious exegetes as Philo. It is the stories and thought-patterns which must lie behind these passages and the Gospel story — not Philo's ingenious intellectual interpretation.

We may fairly assume, then, that concepts of a divine power favouring certain outstanding individuals — especially kings and leaders, but also later philosophers and religious teachers — were still quite real for people in Hellenistic-Roman Egypt at the time of Christian beginnings. Such figures were invested with an aura of divine origination, and brought about the ever-repeated renewal of the life of the world which was fundamental to Egyptian religious feeling. The Pharaohs were long gone, but Roman Emperors still tried to lay claim to that aura of divinity. Luke may well have seen in Jesus the result of a divine 'begetting,' albeit purified through the influence of Jewish thought from any trace of sexual generation: a virgin birth.

On close inspection, then, the Hellenistic-Egyptian conception of a divine child does indeed run remarkably parallel in many ways to the older version of virgin birth presented by Matthew. Both sets of ideas are centrally concerned with the continuing divine presence in the world.

Matthew draws upon the Saoshyant-legend with its virgin-birth theme in order to present Jesus as the climax of God's age-long caring for humanity, sending them prophetic reminders and teachers whenever times seemed to be darkest. The legends had already spoken of a universal World-Saviour who would come at the end of the sequence, and apocalyptic Judaism had already adapted it to Jewish ideas. The providence of the Holy Spirit brought it all to fulfilment with the virginal birth of Jesus and his baptism in the Jordan, when that Spirit was poured out upon him.

Luke draws upon birth-legends belonging to the sphere of the Succession Myth of ancient Egypt, according to which the divinity present in each and every Pharaoh did not die but was mystically reborn in each new ruler, who became Horus as his predecessor became the dead god, Osiris. Perhaps too the stories carried associations of death and resurrection, which would be evocative in the Christian setting of Luke's Gospel. But again there had been developments preparing the way. Jewish visionary writings which were attributed to the Sibyls show that in the Hellenistic period there were many in their community who longed for a new 'king from the sun,' like the old Pharaohs. After the dreadful time of the Roman Civil Wars, which engulfed the whole Mediterranean world, there was a yet more fervent longing for peace and renewal. Augustus aspired to fulfil that dream. But in a much deeper sense it was to be fulfilled by Christianity. Christianity was to speak of a new way that God could be present in the hearts of men, different from dependence on a god-inspired ruler, more direct and personal than in the ancient world. The virgin-born Jesus of Luke's Gospel is already a manifestation of that presence making itself felt. In a way that was not so for Matthew, Luke's newly-born Jesus is a divine child inaugurating a new era in God's dealings with humanity.

7. Virgin Birth — The Mystery

An overshadowing power

From the very first stages of this study we have been forced to refer again and again to ideas from 'esoteric' sources, like the Essenes, Therapeutae or the Egyptian Hermetists. It very quickly became apparent that in Judaism, in particular, there had been at the time Christianity began certain groups which aspired to bring about a new age of religious thought, in which Jewish monotheism would play a central part but which would fulfil the hopes of all humanity, including the gentiles such as Romans and Greeks. They believed that although the different religions were outwardly separate systems with their separate histories, they were on a deeper level all fragments of the original divine wisdom. They did not see themselves as mixing together different religious ideas, but as restoring that primal unity. It was only the anti-divine spiritual powers, the Fallen Angels, who had corrupted human knowledge, giving it a secondary, pagan reality. The esotericists' mission was attended with a certain danger, therefore, that they would fall prey themselves to those demonic, Luciferic powers and lose the central Jewish core of monotheistic belief. Of this they were well aware. Nevertheless, what they were convinced they were actually doing was to rediscover the original, pure sources of the partial, corrupted pagan wisdom. The pagan world would then itself recognize the fuller truth it had aspired to express. The Essenes clearly believed that a meeting of minds and hearts on that level was essential to the future, and that in the light of the central teachings of Judaism all wisdom would flow together. They believed that they themselves already possessed that wisdom, and that they were the advance guard of the new age, which would shortly unfold in external reality too.

All would be finally clear when the Royal and Priestly Messiahs came.

The esoteric search for the synthesis of ideas behind pagan and biblical wisdom alike was the crucible for the meeting of minds which generated many of the extraordinary images and concepts we have explored. The symbolism of the virgin birth is embedded in this rich complex of religious imagery and ideas, much of it originally pagan but enriched through contact with the Jewish milieu: ideas about the cycles of time, about God's providential guidance of the cosmos and history, about humankind's salvation. We have also touched many times upon the suggestion of ritual processes in the esoteric milieu — rites of rebirth, or sacred marriage. Essenes and Therapeutae practised extensive rites of initiation, like the Mysteries of the pagan world. So we cannot avoid the question any longer. The concept of the virgin birth was associated with a new age, a new revelation, a reappearing Prophet, a World-Saviour, a mystical divine child: but what did it mean in itself? We now know the setting. But why did those who spoke from that esoteric milieu describe the decisive event which would bring in the new age as a virgin birth? Despite Philo's ingenious effort to read it into the Bible, they did not derive it from thence, but certainly from the Mysteries that had now flowed into Judaism in esoteric form. What happened in those Mysteries that could prompt such an extraordinary symbolism?

A first clue is the language employed by Luke in his 'annunciation' to Mary of the divine child (1:35):

> The angel answered:
> The Holy Spirit shall come upon you,
> and the power of the Most High shall overshadow you.

This 'overshadowing,' as Norden and others have pointed out, is Mystery-language. It is used by Philo and brought together with Old Testament ideas in his usual fashion, but in all versions it alludes to a very typical, even fundamental experience of the Mysteries: the experience of a higher power, a spiritual presence. When that presence makes itself felt, the ordinary, this-world orientated mind is darkened exactly as if we found ourselves suddenly in the shadow of a greater being looming over us. We are 'overshadowed,' darkened in our ordinary self, because we experience a sense of a greater and higher being, a divine entity.

In the Mysteries those who were being initiated went through the most amazing, and sometimes dramatic processes. Plutarch reveals some of their secrets — though only some — in various passages of his essays. He characterizes the process as a wandering in darkness, before being suddenly illuminated with a mystic-supernatural light. First we lose our bearings, our ordinary mind's sense of orientation, as if we were going astray in utter darkness; into that experience comes the revelation of higher being, the divine light. Though we know little about the details of ancient initiation in the Mysteries, we do know that it was an overwhelming religious experience, and that those who went through it believed they had had an actual glimpse of Eternity. They had known their own eternal being too, and could 'die with a better hope.' What we do know about the Mysteries is that the candidates were aided in touching the central experience of 'illumination' in every way possible — through symbols, meditation, prayer, ritual, and the recital of the sacred myths which reproduce, of course, the essential course of the process they themselves will go through, in the footsteps of the gods.

Aristotle comments that those who went through the Mysteries did not 'learn anything' — i.e. it was not a matter of conscious processes — but were 'moulded.' Without claiming to offer a profound psychological interpretation of the Mysteries, it is obvious enough that in the events which took place powerful psychic forces which normally remain unconscious were brought into play, 'overshadowing' but also then reintegrating the personality. They were completely reshaped. Indeed the initiates often characterize their experience as a new birth: from that point they are a new and different person. They are also aware of more than our ordinary consciousness, our conventional thinking, can contain. They experience an expansion of awareness, a greater being that is born from their ordinary self.

The Mystery-experience is a sort of opposite pole to dreaming. Dreams are very prominent in the Gospel of Matthew, at least in the infancy chapters, where Joseph is repeatedly guided by the angel in dreams, the Magi are warned in a dream, etc. A dream in this sense is an intimation of a reality beyond our ordinary sphere of knowledge, too: but it clothes itself in images from our familiar world, pictures and forms which echo the ordinary mind's apprehension of things around us in the physical world. A spiritual content (the 'Angel') enters into the sphere of our life when the waking ego is out of the way, asleep. But in the 'overshadowing' experience of the Mysteries, the waking self is present but its ordinary content is displaced. The bright, waking world is left behind as the mind crosses over into the spiritual world. It would be quite wrong to think of the 'darkening of reason,' as Philo describes it, as in any way a dimming of the mind. Indeed, on the other side we experience a dazzling illumination — so much so that the ordinary world's brightest day seems to be darkness. Thus the Hermetic writings speak of the outer brightness in paradoxical language as 'the dark light.' The mystic darkness is the leaving behind of the sensory reality, not a falling asleep. The experience of 'overshadowing' is the inverse, the exact mirror-picture opposite of dreaming.

Beautiful as they are, it is possible to be too much influenced by the masterpieces of painting which have depicted the famous scene of the Annunciation. Perhaps we recall Fra Angelico's harmonies of movement and repose in the figures of the arriving angel and the pensive Virgin, the symbolic colours, blues and pinks, and the balance even of the Fall and the Redemption shown by the backdrop of Adam, Eve and the apple. The whole seems as though it were made for visual representation. It is almost a physical shock, therefore, when Margaret Barker points out that Luke's account of the scene contains nothing at all about Mary seeing an angel. In the biblical description, there is no visual reference at all. Mary hears the message of an angel, addressed to her; and it may be that her extraordinary uncertainty 'what kind of greeting this was' is really meant to suggest that she actually saw nothing at all. She encounters the angel as an invisible, inexplicable voice calling her favoured with God. Luke is elsewhere keen on visions, dreams and signs: the very fact that he does not say here that 'the angel appeared to her and said,' or anything like it, should alert us to the special quality of the scene. Of course, the angelic message is not yet the event of the overshadowing of which he tells her. But it does indicate that we are moving in the realm of experiences which are not to be described in terms of picture and image clothing a spiritual content coming into this world, so much as an exaltation of consciousness to an angelic-spiritual reality. In this way Luke's Gospel is also the polar opposite of Matthew's with its frequent dream-interventions.

Philo has many other interesting things to say about the state of the soul in which the rational self is 'overshadowed.' Crucially, points out Eduard Norden, he tells us that it is in precisely this condition that 'the spirits are able to unite with us.'

The plural is a little disconcerting, since previously we have rather learned from him about the Spirit, which draws near to a pure-minded woman and engenders some great man or thinker. The pagan background to Philo's ideas seems to show through more glaringly in the reference to a plurality of spirits. Moreover, the terminology of 'uniting' with us has a frankly sexual connotation which he elsewhere was at pains to mute. In fact, the Mysteries made free use of the imagery of the sacred marriage, in which a human could be united with a spirit or a deity. The language they use makes clear, even, that the normally unconscious forces which are unleashed to 'mould' or reshape the personality have a specifically sexual charge. The loss of one's limited identity in the release of psychic energies through initiation was experienced as a quasi-erotic union with the powers of the spiritual world, from which a rebirth of that higher self, or greater, overshadowing being, took place. We may begin to understand why the mythology of the virgin birth, even in the New Testament, is set against an implication of ambivalent, even sinful sexual connotations. There are obviously great dangers in releasing such forces except under the proper controls and conditions. Those legends about the Fallen Angels having intercourse with the daughters of men, which were a recurring theme in the prototype stories of Enoch and Noah, are also directly related to these forces. Even the Virgin Mary conceives her child, according to Matthew, under an aura of sinfulness and suspicion in the mind of her 'righteous' husband Joseph. The higher birth of the Mysteries is of course not sinful: but it is a process involving disturbing psycho-sexual forces which if wrongly handled could become instead what was known as the union with the Fallen Angels.

In subsequent Christianity the knowledge of the Mysteries was preserved especially by the so-called Gnostics. Though they were to be ejected from the Church in the coming centuries as heretics, there is widespread agreement among scholars that their ideas played a role in many of the earliest Christian developments. They attributed salvation to *gnosis,* the special kind of knowledge that could only be obtained by the Mystery-process. Many of them considered that the Mystery-knowledge was now made accessible to humanity through Jesus, though often still through special ritual and meditative paths. But for them he could only be the Redeemer inasmuch as he brought that inwardly transformative Mystery-knowledge, or *gnosis.* Neither external historical events, nor mere adherence to particular beliefs, as came to be held by the Church, were otherwise efficacious. We do not need to tarry here to establish the rights and wrongs of their treatment by the Church, nor to deny that if pressed to an extreme their ideas could lose touch with the actual events of Christianity and focus entirely on spiritual insight in a profound but definitely one-sided way. What matters to us is that their ideas were intimately involved in interpreting the events of Christianity in the early stages, and that they inherited and perpetuated some features later lost to the orthodox Church tradition, especially as concerning its links to the Mysteries.

The Gnostics certainly understood the 'overshadowing' experience of the Mysteries. For example the Jewish or semi-Jewish Gnostics called the Mandaeans, whose traditions still survive today, speak of the Redeemer as Manda d'Hayye or 'Knowledge of Life' — the knowledge obtained in the Mysteries. He sends out his awakening cry from the spiritual world, and all earthly glory is darkened:

> A cry rang out over the whole world, the splendour departed from every city. Manda d'Hayye revealed himself to the children of men and redeemed them from darkness into light.

This is exactly the 'overshadowing' experience which is said in the Gospel will come to Mary. The Gnostics also, however, place considerable stress on the dangers of the path from darkness into light. The myths which they recited tell of the prototypical figure of Wisdom (Sophia). In a sense every wise man/woman, or initiate, must become one with her in essence. But there is also in the mythology a fallen Wisdom, or lower Sophia, who dramatizes the dangers and failings of those who do not attain illumination in the correct way. And, curiously, it is in these cautionary stories that we encounter what is in the most literal sense a virgin birth — though it is precisely *not* the true inner birth which was the ideal!

Sophia is characterized in the myths as a lesser divine being, who aspires however to know God and to be creative in imitation of his example. But she wants this experience, it transpires, in an immature way — she wants it for herself, and not in the selfless way that would alone be the right way of using the spiritual forces with which God has gifted her. She longs to be equal, in other words, to God. The myths express her selfishness and immaturity in several ways: she tries to expand herself to be equal with God, and catastrophically loses her identity because she is not infinite and illimitable as God is; or, in other versions, she wants to create without her divinely appointed consort — called Theletos (Greek for 'willed,' i.e. to be creative in the particular way willed for her by God). The myths are equivalent though they express themselves in several ways. And, either because she cannot become equal with God, or because she is trying to create without her consort, she gives birth to an attempted creative offspring: but it is formless, immature, an abortion. It falls down from the spiritual regions into a dark realm of its own.

What an amazing agreement of themes, and total reversal of perspective, on the concept of virgin birth! Sophia does indeed give birth out of herself alone, virginally. And she has contact with no lesser Father for her offspring, but opens herself up to God alone. Yet the result is a horror story. The myth encapsulates all the dangers of the path of mystical awakening and higher consciousness. Unless we approach the Mysteries in the purest, most selfless state of mind, our egotism will corrupt the forces we unleash into the most destructive and fiendish parody of true spiritual enlightenment. Indeed, the Gnostics' mythology explains that this is the very reason for the existence of our fallen and imperfect world. For in their cosmic interpretation of the Sophia-myth, the abortive child/creation which falls down into the dark material depths is indeed the first form of this lower world in which we live. In short, it is because humanity has not yet been able to rise to selfless, creative imitation of God, that instead we have created a world of alienation, externality, lovelessness, an abortive creation. In the myth, Sophia herself — or at least the lower part of her, the egotistical part — is trapped within the material domain she has caused to come into being. The abortion becomes a tyrannical monster who thinks he is God, and in a sense is God to the blinkered minds of those inhabiting this fallen reality, who can likewise see nothing beyond their own self. He begets angels in turn, and these defile the mother, Sophia — a version, perhaps, of what was elsewhere described as union with the Fallen Angels. Or at least, it seems to those who are trapped and blinkered here below that she has been raped; nevertheless in her eternal essence she continues to be characterized as 'the virgin whom no power has defiled.'

Such mythology, for all its resonances of virginity, being fecundated by God, danger of subjection to the 'fallen angels' or archons, and similar agreements in subject matter with the virgin-birth story, may seem a long way from the New Testament. The heretical Gnostic version would once upon a time — or actually, not so long ago! — simply have been dismissed as a heretical fantasia that had later been spun on the Christian themes. But the idea that myths like the ones which feature in Gnosticism have a close connection with Christian origins cannot be dismissed. In chapter 2 of his letter to the group of Christians at Philippi, for instance, Paul tries to explain what the coming of Christ really meant. It meant God manifesting himself here below, that is obvious: but not, as one might wrongly imagine, in a powerful way, as though Jesus were to announce to trembling mortals 'I am God;' rather (and translating rather literally):

> though being divine in form, he did not think gaining
> equality with God was something to be seized hold of, but
> actually made himself nothing, taking the form of a servant,
> and took on an existence like that of human beings ... he
> made himself humble even to the point of death — a death
> on a cross!

Paul seems very tentative here, or is perhaps giving his version of some Christian affirmation of faith — it seems to many scholars as though he is alluding to something, taking it up, paraphrasing it in his own way. And at the same time the ideas which emerge appear to run parallel or in conscious antithesis to the Sophia-myth. In the warning tale, she did indeed want to set herself as equal to God in creation, and did not have the humility to play her creative role as a 'servant' of the greater whole and humanity. Her offspring even more literally 'seized' Godhead by becoming ruler of the material, fallen world he had created. Obviously Paul did not, and could not know the late Valentinian version — but perhaps both are building on a common Wisdom-foundation? In his first letter to the Corinthian Christians, Paul uses quite extraordinary language, speaking of receiving a revelation 'as was made to the abortion,' which seems to refer directly to the Gnostic myth. (The bowdlerized rendering: one 'who was born out of due time,' is a softening of the language that probably cannot, in strict terms, be got from the Greek, which almost certainly has the noun rather than the related verb-form that would be required.)

In this extraordinary symbolism, Gnostics and Christians seem to be struggling with the new context of the Mystery-experience. For in Christianity it is repeatedly to be observed that the spiritual struggles and insights which were formerly gone through by the community, embodied in its traditions or emblazoned in the authority-figures of kings or priests, are increasingly the domain of the individual. Gnostic attitudes, which are based on a continuation of the old Mystery-ideas, stress the dangers of thereby bringing in egotism, one-sidedness, incoherence: to be an individual is to give birth to oneself, to try to by-pass one's dependence on the cosmos. But Christianity, starting from a similar continuity with the older Mysteries of the divine, affirms the more modern sense that we must live our own lives. The sort of 'virgin birth' which Philo describes, where we allow the spiritual world to unite with us, but keep ourselves 'virginal,' absorbing the Mystery-experience as a sort of personal education, already points the same way. Christianity goes even further in suggesting that we can thus avoid the dangers of egotism and one-sidedness, and find our way to inner rebirth in our personal quest for God. In the past, people had given themselves up to forces greater than themselves — a community and its traditions, or a pattern of life like that of Egypt. Now it could become individual experience; but then we take Christian responsibility for keeping ourselves pure — 'virgin' — as well.

Rudolf Steiner is one of the few to have grasped this aspect of the Christian development. His understanding of the connection between Christianity and humankind's spiritual evolution led him already to the realization that the virgin birth is not a singularity of Jesus, but a Mystery which has significance for all of us on the spiritual journey we must consciously undertake as Christians. In fact, rather remarkably, he declares that it is a matter which will one day become a recognized truth of natural science — in harmony, as he says, with what will be a valid 'spiritual science.' For it refers to that in us which is not derived from mother and father. He was of course well aware that science currently endeavours to establish,

> through examination of substances under the microscope, which attributes have been genetically transmitted by the male and which by the female, and the researchers are satisfied when they consider it can be proved that the entire human being is produced in this way. But natural science itself will eventually be compelled to recognize that only a part of the human being is determined by the genetic intermingling of male and female, and that however precisely the product of one or the other may be known, the whole nature of a person in the present phase of evolution cannot be explained by this joint inheritance.*

As a matter of fact, many scientists do come to similar conclusions, and increasingly acknowledge that the mere genetic constitution is not in any way a substitute for factors of developmental history, upbringing, education, — for our individual history — which will equally radically affect what we become.

For Steiner, what is shaping the material of our given nature is the ego. Since we are just at the moment in the mode of mentioning parallels, it may be worth adding that an increasingly admired philosopher, Richard Swinburne, has recently argued in terms very close to Steiner's that the process of human development is best understood as effected by a non-material agent — though he calls it by the more general term 'soul' — which makes of us

---

* Steiner, (1988) *The Gospel of Luke,* London and New York 1988, pp.188f.

what it needs in order to manifest itself in our physical nature.
But back to Rudolf Steiner:

> There is in everyone something that does not arise from
> genetics but is, so to speak, a 'virgin birth,' something that
> flows into the process of development from a quite different
> source. Something unites with the genetic material that is
> *not* derived from father and mother, something which yet
> belongs to and is destined for him. It is something which
> is poured into his ego-nature, and which can be ennobled
> through the Christ-principle.
>
> That in human beings which unites with the Christ-prin-
> ciple in the course of evolution is 'virgin born' and — as
> natural science will one day come to recognize through
> its own methods — this is connected with the momentous
> transition accomplished at the time of Christ Jesus.

Almost uniquely in modern times, Rudolf Steiner has realized the reference of the 'virgin born' to something which every
human being now shares in, and which can have that special creative relationship to Christ. And the transition he refers to is one
we can witness vividly played out in the transformation of the
Mysteries now partly opened to our gaze by new discoveries and
texts. Christianity overturned the ancient sense that becoming an
individual could only mean breaking away from the wholeness,
the universality of the divine: in its more esoteric forms it asserts
that we have each something within us which can carry the role
of the Mysteries, which can become a bearer of the divine — a
virgin-born higher self.

The most fascinating evidence of this transition, and of the
shared background and parting of the ways between Christianity
and Gnosticism, comes from another of the newly discovered
Gospels from Nag Hammadi: the *Gospel of Philip*.

A *star came down*

Though not rediscovered until 1945, the *Gospel of Philip* was probably compiled in the second century of our era. Compiled is not exactly the right word, because the text most likely evolved from traditions and formulae, some ritualistic and some narrative, some teaching: and it was most plausibly the 'catechism' for those being inducted into Christian life in Antioch. As they came to share in Christian life, through baptism, and the other rituals, they would be read the material, explanatory or mysterious, which made sense of what was happening, and instructed in the spiritual dimension of it all. After gaining a certain level of understanding, they would be permitted to share the holiest sacrament, the eucharist. What we might not immediately expect, however, is that there were still higher levels of instruction and rite: for instance, the Christian community evidently consisted not only of living Christians, but also those who had died, and probably the holiest sacrament of all was the 'redemption'-rite, at once a funeral service and a way of accompanying the dead in spirit to their heavenly goal. We should not be too surprised at this, for many Christian groups first used to meet at the tombs of holy men or martyrs, as in the Catacombs in Rome. The subsequent architecture of a Christian Church is actually based fundamentally on the design of a funeral monument. And related to the idea of becoming so spiritual that one can share somehow in the life of heavenly souls, there is the well-known revival (possibly from early Christian sources) of celebrating the *consolamentum* or 'consolation for the dead' for a living Cathar, one who has died to the world, in the later Middle Ages.

The initially confusing sequence of material in the *Gospel,* set out in short paragraphs, starts to fall into place when we relate it to the community's several sacraments of baptism, anointing, marriage, eucharist and redemption; and still more when we realize that they are not just intended for the several situations that require them, but constitute a 'progress of the soul,' which must strive ever higher in order to comprehend the mysteries associated with each of the stages of life. Striking similarities exist to the cultic mysteries of the Mandaean Gnostics, and also to the celebrated Mithraic Mysteries where participation in the rites was strictly determined by attaining a sequence of spiritual 'grades,' much like Freemasonry. The Mandaean rites, which were still being performed in living memory, were learned and studied by the visiting scholar Lady Stefana Drower. They are all variations upon baptism — so that, for example, the bride on her wedding-day is ceremoniously dunked alongside her husband in the river 'Jordan' (as the ritual water-source is always called). The *Gospel of Philip* rites may similarly have overlapped, and built up into a 'super-rite,' i.e. with the higher ones requiring a preliminary baptismal purification, anointing, etc. before leading to higher things. The *Gospel of Philip*'s marriage or 'Wedding Chamber' rite, when used in this way, is the rite of becoming a 'higher Christian' — or, indeed, even more: 'For this one is no longer a Christian, but a Christ' (Saying 67). It signifies the overcoming of inner dualities, the 'marriage' of inner energies, and the birth of a higher consciousness. Henceforth, the initiated person is intimately joined with Christ and lives out of his life. Without doubt the ritual could be used in the community as a marriage-service, and would be understood as raising the couple to a new level of the Christian life. (They were correcting a stage of the Fall, when Eve separated from Adam, bringing 'death ... and all our woe' as a later poet said.) The *Gospel* explains at length that the ritual prevents the bad spirits which may be present in sexuality from troubling the soul (Saying 61); here again we have an equivalent of the Fallen Angels. But evidently the 'higher Christian' could attain that inner condition of purification, be initiated into a higher and more integrated spiritual life, by marrying Wisdom. The higher rite is 'for free men and virgins,' and presumably after taking it they would take no earthly partner.

Now all that we learn from the *Gospel of Philip* might seem no nearer to proving our case for the link between the Gospels and Gnostic-Mystery ideas. The attainment of *gnosis* through rebirth, leading to a direct sense of one's own divine being or union with Christ, as practised (probably) in second-century Antioch, appears precisely to lead off once again into Gnostic extravagances, as the orthodox would call them. And certainly there are numerous traces of the Gnostic mythology concerning the Virgin Sophia, and her lower split-personalities (Echamoth, Echmoth, etc., cf. Hebrew *Chokmah,* Wisdom). Originally when it was discovered, many researchers jumped to the conclusion that the *Gospel of Philip* was a Valentinian Gnostic treatise, with only external accommodation to the mainstream Christian message. But in-depth study has proved them mistaken. For it has increasingly been noticed that its themes and formulae are intimately related to the central line of development of the sacraments and catechetical instruction in the early Christian Church. While on the other hand, the evidence for its provenance from the Gnostic school of Valentinus has come to look more and more shaky. Most of the central concepts of Valentinus' special form of Gnosticism are missing. There *is* a somewhat parallel account in the Fathers concerning particular Valentinians who mixed, it is true, very similar ideas with typical references to the 'Aeons' of their master's system — but that simply makes the lack of any mention of the Valentinian Aeons in *Philip* the more remarkable. Surely it is more probable that a group of Gnostics used *Philip* or something like it, and interpreted it in the Valentinian mode, adding references to their system? That would make sense; but the motive for a Gnostic group creating a *Gospel,* starting from Valentinianism but then purging it of any reference to the central Valentinian idea of the Aeons is impossible to understand. Moreover, some technical usages which *Philip* shares with Valentinianism, such as the cosmological use of the term 'Middle,' are not in fact used in precisely the Valentinian way. Here yet again it transpires that the Gnostics share some measure of common ground with the early development of Christianity. Only later did they give it a distinctive unorthodox twist.

Equally one could say that only later was Christianity given a distinctively orthodox twist. Though by later standards of

orthodoxy *Philip* is full of unusual ideas, there is nothing to give
the impression within the document that it belongs to a special
group. There are discussions with other Christian views, e.g.
over the resurrection — but they are apparently between different
viewpoints in the Church, and are not defined as the difference
between those with special knowledge (the Gnostics) and those
who have only belief. The aim is to bring the individual being
inducted to a clear understanding of the view affirmed by the
Philip-community, whatever else he might have heard.

By the fourth century, when the Nag Hammadi Library was
put together, a work like the *Gospel of Philip* could only be used
in 'heretical' circles. But earlier, it is clear, it had been used in
an eastern Church which did not regard itself as a special, dis-
senting or Gnostic group. It defines itself only over against the
'Hebrews,' who are either the non-Christian Jewish community
or Christians who still kept to circumcision and Jewish practices,
and speaks of the need for love and goodness to be shown even
to those outside the Church. There is every reason to regard it
as a mainstream type of Church for its time. The focus on the
Mystery-rites had not yet been suppressed or made the preserve
of marginal groups. In some ways *Philip*'s theology anticipates
the great Antiochene theologies of the 'two natures,' and there is
clear knowledge of Syriac or Aramaic words, though the document was presumably written in the *lingua franca*, Greek. The
great Christian centre of Syrian Antioch naturally presents itself
as the home for such a tradition.

It is often thought that the Gospel of Matthew might likewise come from Antioch. We must not put too much weight on
the idea, because Antioch was such a cosmopolitan centre that
several quite different lines of development could have evolved
there. (The Gospel of Luke too has frequently been thought to
be Antiochene.) However, we are on solid ground in marking
the following connections. Where the *Gospel of Philip* shares
material with the New Testament tradition, it is almost always
material in common with Matthew. (There is only one 'erratic
block,' namely the parable of the Good Samaritan, which is

referred to in Saying 111 — and that story, of course, belongs to the special material found in Luke.) And — significantly for our investigation — there is a striking passage about a star. The story of the star of the Magi, moreover, which basically belongs to the special material in Matthew, is mentioned in particular by one of the earliest Church writings outside the New Testament, namely the first-century letters of Ignatius of Antioch. The similarities between the passage in *Philip* and that in Ignatius have led to the theory of a common background.

Ignatius is one of the 'Apostolic Fathers,' or very early group of Christian writers who were still in time to hear the apostles of Jesus pass down the message in person. They have always been highly valued by the Church. Ignatius of Antioch shares, however, many of the somewhat unorthodox influences which appear in *Philip*. In other words, he is definitely Gnostic in tendency by the Church's later standards. He uses Gnostic contrasts of Light and Darkness, references to Mysteries, and secrets hidden 'in the silence of God' from the 'Prince of this World' and the uninitiated. But this only tells us that he belongs to the world of pre-orthodox Christianity, not that he belonged to any marginal Gnostic group. He evidently played a part in organizing the early Church, and his strong opposition to those who wanted many Judaistic features retained and who could not believe that God had really come down to earth in Jesus earned the gratitude of the later Fathers, together with a place in history only less than that of the apostles themselves as a fountainhead of the Christian tradition.

Among the concealed Mysteries, we find, is Mary's virginity, as well as her actual giving birth to the Messiah. So he writes to the community in Ephesus (Ignatius, *Ephesians* 19), and his stress on these events as crucial to the Christian faith certainly links him to Matthew. We surmised that Matthew already took over the legends about Jesus' birth from the community for which he wrote, since they otherwise play no part in his Gospel. Perhaps Ignatius belongs to the same early line, though he most probably knows Matthew's Gospel too, since he also alludes e.g. to the anointing of Jesus (Matt.26:7). He treats the Matthaean episode, however, very freely:

> Up in the heavens a star gleamed out, more brilliant than
> all the rest; no words could describe its lustre, and the
> strangeness of it left men bewildered. The other stars and
> the sun and moon gathered round it in chorus, but this star
> outshone them all.

It betokens the end of the pagan Mysteries, tainted by super-stition and evil magic however, their disappearance appar-ently leaves men bewildered. For as he has explained, the new Christian 'Mysteries of a loud shout' were still utterly secret and unknown until now, when they can safely be proclaimed. In his version, the Prince of this World plays the would-be persecuting role of Matthew's Herod, but no more than Matthew's wicked king was he able to fathom the unexpected appearance of the child who will defeat his age-old empire. Ignatius' interpretation rather confirms that the Matthaean Herod is a basically mythical figure, an age-old dragon rather than a historical client-king.

The mythical emphasis continues as, amidst the cosmic 'cho-rus' God prepares to take human form:

> God was even now appearing in human form to bring in a
> new order, that of life without end. Now, that which had
> been perfected in divine deliberation began to be realized.
> All creation was thrown into a ferment over this plan for
> the utter destruction of death.

Ignatius rightly understands that the virgin birth and the star are indicators that Jesus is to bring in a new age, and a new rev-elation. In his more mythic version, note too, it is not only 'all Jerusalem' that was disturbed along with Herod/Prince of This World, but the entire creation. Compared with Ignatius, Matthew has gone far to 'historicize' the mythological resonances and to domesticate them into homely legends that apply to the infant

Jesus. Ignatius evidently thinks that from these once silent but now vocal and shining Mysteries, the virgin birth and the star, will emerge the future and truly divine revelation leading to eternal life. He also mentions the baptism and the passion — but it is the Matthaean special Mysteries that take his attention and awaken his imagination.

If Ignatius takes us back to cosmic and mythological pictures behind the Gospel-story, the *Gospel of Philip* introduces dramatically the dimension of cult and ritual. But some of its phrases are remarkably close to Ignatius. When Ignatius describes Jesus' baptism, he says (*Ephesians* 18) that 'he submitted to baptism, so that by his passion he might sanctify water;' and *Philip* says 'By perfecting the water of baptism, Jesus emptied it of death. Thus we (Christians) go down into the water, but not unto death' (Saying 109). When Ignatius describes the birth of Jesus as providentially brought about by God in secret so that the Ruler of This World did not know of it, he agrees with the *Gospel* that the mythological 'world-rulers.' i.e. powers of darkness, were deceived, and 'the Holy Spirit brought about everything through them as he wished' (Saying 16; cf. 34: 'for they [the evil powers] are blind through the Holy Spirit'). One of the central Mysteries of the *Gospel* is the virginity of Mary (Saying 17); but the meaning of it can easily be misunderstood:

> Some have said, 'Mary conceived by the Holy Spirit.' They
> are in error; they do not understand what they say. When
> did a woman ever conceive by a woman? Mary is the virgin
> whom no power has defiled.

Philip thus agrees with Matthew that the birth of Jesus was a providential working of the Holy Spirit, and that the story in Matthew 1–2 is wrongly interpreted by some Christians as that of God 'begetting' a Son. The Holy Spirit is a 'woman,' the feminine hypostasis of God, and the *Gospel* thereby hints that it agrees with the Jewish-Christian idea that Jesus was on a higher level, through his baptismal reception of its influx, a 'child of the

Holy Spirit;' but that is nothing to do with his virgin birth. At the climactic moment of his baptism, one can indeed say there was a divine birth (Saying 81):

> Jesus revealed (in the) Jordan the fullness of the kingdom of heaven. He who (came into being) before the All was begotten again.

Jesus has, however, also an earthly father as well as an earthly mother. And in addition he has his 'Father in heaven,' just as in the person of the Holy Spirit he has a divine mother. Here the *Gospel* anticipates the later Antiochene theology of the distinct 'two natures,' human and divine, which are joined in Jesus. And even more remarkably, the *Gospel* makes it clear that the mystery of Jesus' 'virgin birth' is nothing to do with some literalistic idea that he had no human father on earth.

Mary, however, is identified with 'the virgin whom no power has defiled,' and this, as we have seen, is a phrase that belongs to the Gnostic mythology. The 'Virgin' is here, as in Philo and elsewhere, equated with the Sophia, or Wisdom who, with God's aid, gives birth to the higher self in us. The *Gospel of Philip* stresses, again rather like Philo, that the defilement by the 'powers' or fallen angels is far removed from the true representative of this figure — that she is virginal. 'The powers have defiled themselves' (Saying 17). So it is for anyone who is duly prepared for the unleashing of unconscious forces, which if one is not purified will indeed wreak terrible vengeance as in the Gnostic myth. The spiritual world unites with us in a quasi-sexual way, but one must have become spiritual first, just as animal mates with animal, human with human (Saying 113).

As the virgin Sophia, Mary is even rather amazingly seen as a triple goddess, at once the Mary who is Jesus' mother, also her sister Mary, and Mary Magdalene, Jesus' sinful companion whom he nevertheless loved greatly. Here we probably have a direct transposition from the Mysteries like those of Eleusis, where the cultic goddess was represented both as earth-Mother

(Demeter) and fertility-goddess (Koré, 'the Maiden'), and also
in a dark aspect (Hecate, or Persephone 'the destroyer' as death-
goddess). Like the corn-god of Eleusis bringing the cultivation
of wheat, so Jesus is also identified as the divinity who brought
the true food to humanity — bread, which is consecrated in the
eucharist (Saying 15). Antioch had a special connection to the
Eleusinian Mysteries, which may have given these ideas a special
relevance. But the *Gospel* is not far removed here from popular
Christian piety, which very rapidly recognized 'Mary' in images
of the goddess Isis suckling her child Horus, or in the virgin
Goddess whose image had fallen from heaven at Ephesus, and
whom the Greeks called after their Artemis.

To become one in essence with a goddess, or in more Judaic
terms, with Wisdom — that after all was a well-known goal of the
Mysteries, and wisdom's 'child' is the spiritual new existence, the
Christ-self which is born from divine illumination. Wisdom, the
Gospel explains, is barren (outwardly, that is to say: she is virginal, 'undefiled' by the powers of the world) — yet her children
are many. They are the virtues and good deeds that the regenerate
Christian brings into the world, very much as in Philo's allegory
of the higher learning. For the *Gospel of Philip* higher knowledge
of the Mysteries belongs only with an existential transformation,
a metamorphosis of the ordinary self into a Christ-self. Mary's
experience of angelic foreknowledge that she would be overshadowed and give birth to such a child, Sarah in Philo representing
procreative Wisdom, Aseneth ritually humbling herself in order
to be joined in a prophetic-spiritual marriage with the 'Son of
God' (= Joseph) in the story from the Therapeutae sect: these are
all versions of the Mystery theme. In the *Gospel* it is described
in terms at once highly ritual and symbolic, yet also very close
to Matthew. We come now to the heart of its description (Saying
82):

> If it is fitting to utter a Mystery: the Father of the All united
> with the Virgin who came down, and a Star shone forth for
> him on that day. He appeared in the great Wedding Chamber.

> Therefore his body, which came into being on that day, came
> forth from the Wedding Chamber. As he who came into
> being from the bridegroom and the bride, Jesus established
> the All in it by these means. And it is fitting for each of his
> disciples to enter into his rest.

The translation from the Coptic in which the Nag Hammadi
texts survives posed a number of problems, and the allusion to the
star was missed in the earlier versions. But the whole Saying has
to do with heavenly reality coming down to earth. The Wedding
Chamber, in which the illumination of the initiate takes place,
becomes an image of the universe, like a Mithras-temple. It is
a place on earth where one could find the reality of Star. The
Mithraic rites also included a 'Bride'-initiation, involving baptism and the revelation of a 'new light.' The *Gospel of Thomas*
mentions the Wedding Chamber, in connection with the elect or
'unified ones,' who have transcended inner divisions and made
'the two become one.' Christian and pagan Mysteries here still
stand very close.

The Star shining out, the mystic marriage of the Virgin and
the Father of the All, and the invitation for those who would
be disciples to follow and share in the 'rest,' the fulfilment:
Matthew's Gospel-story, with the virgin-mother and the star of
the Magi, is not far away. Indeed it seems beyond doubt that
Matthew and Ignatius and the *Gospel of Philip* show a developing tradition. The birth of Jesus is made the basis for a new
form of the Mysteries, bringing eternal life into the sphere down
here below. The imagery of the virgin birth is elaborated within
a Mystery-cult that becomes an important form of Christianity
in the Hellenistic East. Whether or not he too wrote in Antioch,
Luke presents many parallels to this development also: more
evidence that the *Gospel of Philip* originally belonged within the
mainstream of Christian evolution.

A pagan Mystery is transformed into one which enabled the
early Christians to experience the reality of the *divine birth* of
Jesus here on earth — so there had to be development on both

sides. But what is important is the fact that the virgin birth was here something that could be grasped, in its inner reality, in a transformation of consciousness in the ritual- and life-setting of early Christianity. By failing to look at the wider language and symbolism in which it is embedded, later Christians and even scholars have made the virgin birth a singularity — a miraculous but rather meaningless demonstration that Jesus was just different from everyone else. But the perspective in these restored documents of early Christianity is just the reverse. The virgin birth was indeed the climax of a long history, when the one destined to bring in the new age, the Transfiguration of the Earth, would be born. But that birth had now happened, and it could become the basis of a new experience of divine birth, the birth of the Christ-self which was a 'higher initiation' in early Christianity. No longer a matter of giving oneself up to cosmic forces in a quasi-erotic union, and living in a pre-conscious harmony with the great rhythms of the spirit in nature, as had happened in paganism, the new birth was purified and 'virginal.' The dangers of falling back into the old ways, when it was possible to share in cosmic creativity, are vividly spelled out in the Gnostic myth — even as they are intimated in the warnings of how close the virgin birth stands to sin and the Fallen Angels which recur in the Jewish-esoteric legends. It seems as though the nature of the new synthesis, the new revelation foreseen by the Essenes and their like, had become more personal, more inward, and its God was the One God of Judaism, purely spiritual and transcendent. Yet without sliding back into old cosmic vision, which would now bring Luciferic delusions of grandeur and cosmic abortion, a new rapprochement with the Mysteries was nevertheless found: at its heart was the experience of cosmic reality and spiritual rebirth in a striking new form. It was the virgin birth.

Acknowledgments

The materials of this book have occupied me, in a scholarly and spiritual way, over a good many years. It is therefore only fair to single out for mention first (at least in a collective fashion) those who have had to hear about them more often than the call of duty required. Beyond that, I would still like to refer to the decisive encouragement I received at moments from certain revered authorities on particular aspects of the sources, notably Professor Mary Boyce (University of London) on the Iranian connections of the *Apocalypse of Adam,* Professor Christopher Rowland (University of Oxford) on the Jewish setting of the same work, and Sebastian Brock (University of Oxford) on the Syriac background of the *Gospel of Philip* which also refers to the virgin birth. Needless to say the responsibility for the views expressed is entirely my own.

Another determining piece of encouragement came with the invitation to give a course of lectures at the still quite new Seminar of the Christian Community in Hamburg, in which many of the ideas here set out were touched upon with the opportunity to focus more freely on the questions of the miracles, the relationship of earthly and divine birth in the Gospels of Matthew and Luke, and the nature of the Gospel narratives. Grateful thanks go there above all to Rev. Günther Delbrügger and Rev. Gwendoline Fischer, but also to that fresh generation of students, so diverse and yet contributing through discussion to a harmony of viewpoints with their questions and concerns. I hope that they will accept my admiration and appreciation of their drive, enthusiasm and pioneering work at the Hamburg Seminary, inadequately expressed in the dedication of the book.

Books and Further Reading

CHIEF NON-BIBLICAL SOURCES REFERRED TO:

Joseph and Aseneth (a romance *c.* first century bc or first century ad).

The legend of Noah's birth in the Dead Sea Scrolls and *1 Enoch* (? second century bc).

The story of Melchizedek in *2 Enoch* (uncertain date, ? first/second century ad).

Old Persian legends preserved in later sources.

Symbolic Bible-interpretation of Philo of Alexandria (first century bc – first century ad).

BEST ACCESS FOR MODERN READERS IS THROUGH:

Charlesworth, J.H. (1983, 1985) *The Old Testament Pseudepigrapha,* 2 vols., London. Vol. 1: see *1 Book of Enoch* chs.106–7 for the story of the miraculous birth of Noah; and *2 Book of Enoch* chs.70–2 for the posthumous birth of Melchizedek. Vol.2: see *Joseph and Aseneth* for the story of an angelic visitation, a star and the advent of the 'man of God.'

Levy, R. (ed. trans.) (1967) *Shahnameh. The Epic of the Kings,* London. Mediaeval Persian epic based on ancient legendary traditions. See the stories of Zal and Faridun.

Vermes, Geza (1998) *The Complete Dead Sea Scrolls in English,* Harmondsworth. See especially *The Genesis Apocryphon* (1QApGen) for the story of Noah's scandalous birth.

Welburn, A.J. (1994) *Gnosis. The Mysteries and Christianity,* Edinburgh. See the *Apocalypse of Adam* for the prophecy of a new age as the culmination of a series of revelations through 'the Illuminator' or True Prophet; also contains the *Gospel of Philip* with its mystery of 'virginal birth' for all Jesus' followers.

Winston, D. (ed. trans.) (1981) *Philo of Alexandria. The Contemplative Life, Giants, and Selections,* London.

BACKGROUND READING:

Allinson, D.C. (2001) commentary on Matthew in *The Oxford Companion to the Bible*, Oxford. Especially for the Gospel's historical setting still within Judaism.

Barker, Margaret (2003) *The Great High Priest*, Edinburgh.

Boyce, M. (1984) *Textual Sources for the Study of Zoroastrianism*, Manchester. Includes the legends of the Saoshyant or virgin-born World-Saviour.

Brown, Raymond (1977) *The Birth of the Messiah*, London. Detailed analysis of the infancy stories and the texts of the Gospels.

Cullman, Oscar (1959) *Christology of the New Testament*, London. See the chapter on 'Jesus the Prophet' for this important Jewish-Christian idea.

Edwards, Ormond (1986) *The Time of Christ*, Edinburgh.

Grant, Michael (1999) *The Jews in the Roman World*, London.

Koester, Helmut (1990) *Ancient Christian Gospels*, London and Philadelphia. Especially valuable on the background of 'Stories about Jesus' Birth' particularly Luke.

Meeks, Dimitri and Christine Favard-Meeks (1997) *Daily Life of the Egyptian Gods,* London. Especially for the trial of Osiris, the god who died.

Norden, Eduard (1958) *Die Geburt des Kindes*, Darmstadt. Comprehensive treatment of myths concerning a 'divine child,' the divine birth of the Pharaoh, and including still highly pertinent comments on the Gospel birth-narratives.

Rostovtzeff, M. (1960) *Rome,* Oxford and New York.

Steiner, Rudolf (1997) *Christianity as Mystical Fact*, New York.

— (1986) *The Gospel of Matthew*, London.

— (1988) *The Gospel of Luke*, London. Especially the last lecture for the meaning of the 'virgin birth.'

Welburn, A.J. (ed.) (1997) *The Mysteries. Rudolf Steiner's Writings on Spiritual Initiation*, Edinburgh.

— (2004) *Beginnings of Christianity*, Edinburgh.

— (forthcoming) *Transformations of Religious Experience: The Approach of Rudolf Steiner,* Lampeter.

Index

Work on the Dead Sea Scrolls and other ancient documents has provided new knowledge of the early Christian Church and the messianic sects in the Holy Land around the time of Christ. These texts suggest that the boundaries between early Christian belief, Jewish tradition and the ancient pagan Mysteries are not as well defined as has usually been believed. The Gnostic gospels clearly reveal that early Christianity had a powerful esoteric current, which is also reflected in the New Testament writings of Mark, Paul and, above all, John.

Andrew Welburn reveals a kinship between our own age and the early Christians, and shows how we now have the chance to rediscover their spiritual world and the meaning of Christian beginnings. His companion book, *Gnosis, the Mysteries and Christianity,* contains many of the actual texts discussed in this book.

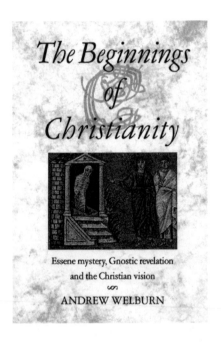

The Beginnings of Christianity

Essene mystery, Gnostic revelation
and the Christian vision

ANDREW WELBURN

www.florisbooks.co.uk

Andrew Welburn presents a selection of the most important early texts from the Dead Sea Scrolls and Nag Hammadi, together with an authoritative and fascinating commentary. He shows how the new insights gained into the writings of the early Christians reaffirm the fundamental mysteries at the heart of Christianity.

A companion volume to *The Beginnings of Christianity.*

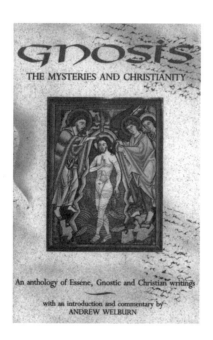

www.florisbooks.co.uk